A Revised Genealogical Account Of The Various Families Descended From Francis Fox, Of St. Germans, Cornwall

Joseph Foster

A

REVISED GENEALOGICAL ACCOUNT

OF THE

VARIOUS FAMILIES DESCENDED FROM

FRANCIS FOX,

OF ST. GERMANS, CORNWALL,

TO WHICH IS APPENDED A PEDIGREE OF THE

Crokers, of Lineham,

AND MANY OTHER FAMILIES CONNECTED WITH THEM.

PRIVATELY PRINTED.

LONDON:

PRINTED FOR THE COMPILER, BY

HEAD, HOLE AND CO., FARRINGDON STREET, AND PATERNOSTER ROW.

1872.

THE DESCENDANTS

OF

FRANCIS FOX,

of St. Germans.

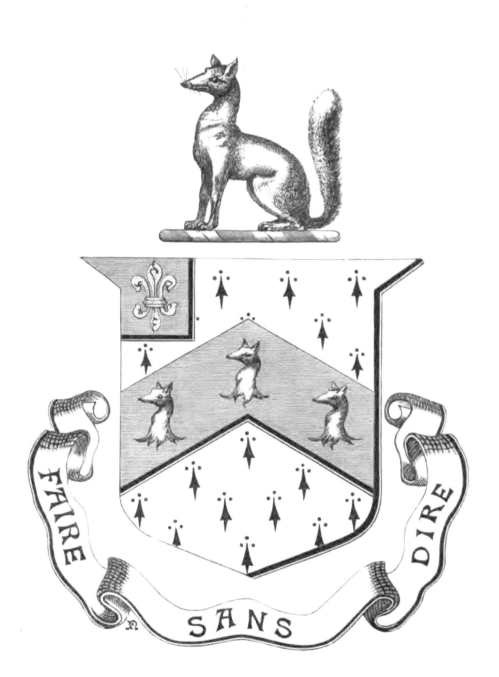

FAIRE SANS DIRE

Contents.

LIST OF PEDIGREES.

	PAGE
Chapline of Wheeling (U.S.)	20
Churchill	25
Collier of Plymouth	16
Cookworthy	18
Copplestone	25
Croker of Lineham	23
Curtis of Moundsville (U.S.)	21
Debell of Looe	19
Dungan of Coleraine (U.S.)	21
Ellicot	22
Fox of Brislington	14
,, Falmouth	12
,, Grove Hill	11
,, Par	11
,, Plymouth	15
,, St. Germans	6
,, Wadebridge	7 & 10
,, Wellington	8 & 9
Hingston of Holbeton	18
De Horne of Stanway	17
Pickering of East Richland (U.S.)	21
Pollard	25
Prideaux of Kingsbridge	17
Tuckett of Devonshire	19
Yeo	25

INTRODUCTORY.

T HIS Pedigree has been enlarged and corrected since its publication in the Second Edition of a work entitled ' A Pedigree of the Forsters and Fosters of the North of England,' in 1871, and has been carefully tested by comparison with a very perfect account of the early generations of the Fox family, as shewn by a Genealogical Chart, made out in the year 1840, by Frances Allen (daughter of John Allen, of Liskeard, and Frances, his wife, *née* Fox, see page 13); and by the personal revision of nearly every family interested in its authenticity.

JOSEPH FOSTER.

ALLONBY VILLA, NEW BARNET,
HERTS, *September*, 1872.

Pedigree of Fox, of Grove Hill, etc.

FOX OF ST. GERMANS.

Burke, in his " History of the Commoners," states "that the
"numerous families of Fox at present residing in the West of
"England sprang from one common ancestor, a Francis Fox, who
"married, 1646, Dorothy Kekewich. Tradition represents him to
"have come from Wiltshire (it is said from the parish of *Farley*,
"or that of *Pitton*), somewhere in 1645, during the commotions
"of the civil war. He is stated to have been descended from
"the same family as the celebrated Sir Stephen Fox, ancestor
"of the Earls of Ilchester and the Lords Holland. It is likewise
"handed down that he was one of seven or eight sons, and that
"others of the same family also came into Devonshire and Corn-
"wall, settling at Plymouth and Looe, but left no sons who
"survived.

"The wife of this Francis Fox was Dorothy Kekewich. She
"was of good family, being a relation of the family of Kekewich
"of Exeter, whose house at Catchfrench, in the parish of St.
"Germans, being then vacant, became their residence on their
"first settling in Cornwall."

FRANCIS FOX and his family, consisting of three sons,
"joined the Society of Friends soon after its first esta-
"blishment in Cornwall. Some of them shared in the sufferings
"that awaited its early members on account of the stand which
"they so resolutely and successfully made for liberty of con-
"science."

He died in 1670, having had three sons :—
(1.) FRANCIS, of whom presently.
(2.) John, died *s. p.* 1651.
(3.) James, married, 1673, Elizabeth Record, of Plymouth, in 1686 removed, with the whole of his family, to Philadelphia : his descendants in the male line soon became extinct.

FRANCIS FOX, of St. Germans, married 1st, in 1671, Joan, daughter of Richard Smith, of Plymouth, by whom he had three sons and two daughters :—
(1.) Francis, died *s. p.* 1686.

(2.) John Fox, died *s. p.* 1692.
(3.) Joshua Fox, died *s. p.* 1698.
(1.) Rachel Fox, married George Hodge, of Plymouth, and left issue.
(2.) Deborah Fox, married Samuel Croker, and left issue.

He married, 2ndly, March 30, 1686, Tabitha, daughter of George Croker, Esq., of the ancient family of Croker of Lineham, county of Devon, who died in 1730. He died 1704, having had three sons and four daughters, viz.—
(1.) Francis Fox, of St. Germans, married, in 1707, Mary, daughter of John Cogger, of St. Austle. They had one son and four daughters, viz.—
    1. Francis Fox, who married, 1738, Hannah Scantlebury, and died 1775; she died in 1782, having had issue, two sons and two daughters—
        i. Stephen Francis Fox, died *s. p.* 1816, aged 74.
        ii. Benjamin Fox (of whom see next page).
        i. Anne Fox, married Thomas Bruce, and left Mary, died *s. p.* 1762; George Fox, died *s. p.* 1796; Marian, died *s. p.*
        ii. Mary Fox, married Peter Cloak, died *s. p.*; married, secondly, Joshua Hancock, died *s. p.*
    1. Tabitha Fox, died *s. p.* 1710.
    2. Mary Fox, married, 1st, to Nicholas Elliott, and had a son and daughter—
        i. Nicholas Elliott, married Honor Hinds, and had an only daughter, Mary, who married Nicholas Berry, and had one daughter, Eleanor, who married — Hemming.
        ii. Mary Elliott, married, 1st, to Nathaniel Ford, and 2ndly, to Edward Richards.
    Mary Elliott married, 2ndly, to John Rice, and had one son— James Rice, who married Rebecca Derry, and had two sons and three daughters—
        i. John Rice.
        ii. Nathaniel Rice.
        i. Catherine Rice.
        ii. Ann Rice.
        iii. Mary Rice.
    3. Anne Fox, married, 1748, to John Gwin, died *s. p.*
    4. Tabitha Fox, died *s. p.* 1725.
(2.) George Fox, of Par, married twice. From the first marriage spring Fox of Wellington, Wadebridge, Kingsbridge, Exeter, &c. From the second marriage (see page 11), those of Falmouth, Plymouth, Gloucester, Brislington, &c. He married, first, 1719, Mary, daughter of Edward Bealing, merchant, of Penryn, and by her had two sons and three daughters—
    1. Edward Fox of Wadebridge (see next page).

2. George Fox, died *s. p.* 1724.
1. Elizabeth Fox, died *s. p.* 1717.
2. Rachel Fox, died *s. p.* 1718.
3. Elizabeth Fox, died *s. p.*
(3.) John Fox, of Plymouth, married twice. He married first, Lovall Applebee; and by her had three sons and one daughter—
    1. John Fox, of Plymouth (of whom see page 15).
    2. Charles Fox, married first, Margaret Jewell, died *s. p.*; second, Sarah Champion, of Bristol, died *s. p.*
    3. James Fox, died *s. p.* 1732.
    1. Jane Fox, died *s. p.* 1729.
John Fox married second, Lydia Berry, and had issue by her, two sons and one daughter—
    1. James Fox, of Plymouth (of whom see page 15).
    2. Berry Fox, married Elizabeth Were, died *s. p.*
    1. Elizabeth Fox, died *s. p.* 1811, aged 66.
(1.) Mary Fox, married 1707, to Andrew Ellicott, of Collumpton (see page 22).
(2.) Sarah Fox, married to Philip Debell, of Looe (see page 19).
(3.) Dorothy Fox, married to Joseph Collier, of Plymouth (see page 16).
(4.) Rachel Fox, died *s. p.* 1706.

BENJAMIN FOX, second son of Francis Fox (see preceding page), married first, 1771, Mary Emmett, and by her had—
(1.) Francis Fox, married, 1803, Ann Sansom. He died at St. Germans, in 1815, having had, with Anne Fox, living unmarried in 1872, another daughter, Mary Fox, married, in 1835, to Edward Anson Crouch, and died at Liskeard, 19 September, 1863, having had with Francis Crouch, living in New York, Marianna Crouch, Lucretia Anson Crouch, and Sophia Crouch, a daughter—
    Frances Anne Crouch, born 21 November, 1837, married 21 September, 1865, to James Grace, and has had four sons and one daughter—
        i. James Edward Grace, born 18 September, 1866.
        ii. Herbert Grace, born 17th November, 1867.
        iii. Shirwin Grace, born 6 June, 1869, and died 17 September, 1871.
        iv. Philip Anson Grace, born 18 October, 1871.
        i. Mary Mabel Grace, born 30 July, 1870, and died 22 August following.
(2.) Joseph Scantlebury Fox (late an officer in the Royal Naval Hospital at Portsmouth), married Jane Lewes Willes, and had issue, eight sons and three daughters, of whom the following died *s. p.*—George Irwin Fox, Benjamin Stephen Francis Fox, who was killed in the Chinese war, in 1842, James Willes Fox, Joseph Bruce Fox, John Willes Fox, Joseph Scantlebury Fox, and Anna Fox.
    6. Cornelius Fox, Captain R.N., married, first, Emma Jarvis, and had a son, Cornelius, who died young. He married, secondly, Fanny Jarvis—no issue.
    8. Henry Treffry Fox, Lieut. Marines, deceased, married Fanny Stephens, who married, secondly. He had with Edward, who died *s. p.*, Charles and Ida Fox.
    2. Jane Fox, married to Thomas Wallis McDonald, Surgeon R.N., now Inspector-General R.N. (who married, secondly, Louisa, widow of Lieutenant C. B. Baskerville, R.N.), and had issue—
        i. Wallis McDonald, surgeon.
        i. Anna McDonald, died *s. p.*
        ii. Mary Tabor McDonald, married to William Ayre, Surgeon R.N., no issue.
        iii. Frances Fox McDonald married to John Holland, Major Royal Marines, and has issue—Charles Theodore Holland, and a daughter born 2 January, 1872.
        iv. Flora McDonald, married to Charles Kealy, and has issue, Mary Kealy.
    3. Elizabeth Treffry Fox, married to Henry Willoughby Taylor, Chaplain R.N., and has had issue, four sons and four daughters—Willoughby Taylor, Henry William Taylor,

Fredk. Taylor, Percy Roger Taylor, Frances D'Esterre Taylor, Aileen Taylor, Kathleen Taylor, and Eveleen Taylor.
    4. Sally Fox, living, unmarried, 1872.
(3.) Benjamin Fox, of Stoke, married Sarah Treffry, and died in 1856, aged 80, having had issue Anna Treffry Fox, deceased; Charles James Fox, married Anna Maria Kerswill, died *s. p.*; Cornelius Willes Fox, of Davenport, deceased, married Sophia Elizabeth Treloar, and had Cornelius Benjamin Fox, now of Scarborough, Sophia Anna Fox, deceased, and Anna Treffry Fox, deceased.
(1.) Susanna Emmett Fox, married to George Hatch, but no issue now survives.
Benjamin Fox, (see preceding col). married, second, Elizabeth Higman, and by her had—
(4.) Stephen Francis Fox—died in 1829 *s. p.* (?)
(2.) Hannah Fox, married to Henry Mewburn, and had three sons and three daughters—1. Henry Benjamin Sorsbie Mewburn, died *s. p.*; 2. George Fox Bruce Mewburn, married Margaret Aitkins, and has had issue—
    i. Henry Fox Mewburn, living, unmarried; ii. Cullen Wordsworth Mewburn, deceased; and Margaret Mewburn, married to Richard Sargent, Barrister-at-Law, and has a son, Cecil, and a daughter.
    3. Henry Simon Mewburn.
    1. Elizabeth Mary Mewburn, married to Rev. Cullen Wordsworth; 2. Dorothy Augusta Mewburn, deceased; 3. Hannah Fox Mewburn, deceased, married to Rev. W. Toms, and has three children, the youngest daughter, Edith, married to C. Ramsay, Esq.

FOX OF WADEBRIDGE.

EDWARD FOX, of Wadebridge, son of George Fox, of Par, by his first marriage (see page 6), married, 1745, Anna, second daughter of Thomas Were, of Wellington, County of Somerset, and had issue five sons and four daughters; viz.—
(1.) George Fox, of Perran Arworthal, married first, Elizabeth Were, and by her had—
    1. Peter Were Fox, born 1779, died 1781.
    1. Elizabeth Were Fox, died 1800.
He married second, Frances James, and died 1816, having had by her three sons and three daughters, viz.—
    2. George Fox, married 1806, Eleanor Rawes. He died 1858 aged 76, having had—
        i. Eleanor Fox, married, at Spiceland, Exeter, 18 October, 1831, to George Braithwaite Crewdson, of Kendal, 2nd son of William Dillworth Crewdson, and has had three sons and five daughters—
            i. William Dillworth Crewdson, born at Kendal, 14th March, 1838; married, at St. Paul's, Knightsbridge, 1st February, 1866, Katherine, daughter of Thomas and Elizabeth Davidson.
            ii. George Crewdson, in Holy Orders, born at Kendal, 18th August, 1840; married, at Bath, 4th January, 1870, Mary Salome Hay Sweet Escott, daughter of the Rev. Hay Sweet Escott and Elizabeth Ball Colling, his wife, and has—
                1. Ethel Maria Crewdson, born at Nottingham, 18th July, 1871.
            iii. Henry Crewdson, born at Kendal, 13th October, 1852.
            i. Eleanor Crewdson, born at Kendal, 19th May, 1833; died 26th May, 1842.
            ii. Anna Rebecca Crewdson, born at Kendal, 29th September, 1834; died 26th May, 1842.
            iii. Maria Jane Crewdson, born at Kendal, 3rd June, 1836.
            iv. Frances Mary Crewdson, born at Kendal, 8th May, 1843; married, at Windermere, 24th Octo-

ber, 1866, to Richard Fletcher Broadrick, R.N., son of George and Jane Broadrick, and has issue—
    1. George Fletcher Broadrick, born at the Wood, Windermere, 5th June, 1870.
  v. Ellen Fox Crewdson, born at Kendal, 13th February, 1845; married, at Windermere, 28th June, 1866, to Frederick Wadsworth, and has issue—
    1. Arthur Frederick Wadsworth, born at Nottingham, 30th June, 1871.
    1. Ellen Beatrice Wadsworth, born at Nottingham, 5th October, 1868.
  ii. Jane Fox, married, at Spiceland, 12th October, 1836, to Thomas Crewdson, 3rd son of William Dillworth Crewdson. He died at Baden Baden, 12th December, 1869, *s. p.*
  iii. Tabitha Fox, married to William Reynolds Lloyd, 4th son of James Lloyd, Esq., of Bingley Hall, co. Warwick.
  iv. Philippa Fox, died *s. p.* at Perran Arworthal.
  v. Frances Elizabeth Fox, died *s. p.* at Perran Arworthal.
3. Edward Fox, died *s. p.* 1806.
4. Robert Phillips Fox, born 1787, married at Kingsbridge, 1812, Sarah, second daughter of George and Anna Prideaux, of Kingsbridge (see p. 18). He died there 1855, having had—
  i. George Fox, born 1815, now of Kingsbridge.
  i. Sarah Prideaux Fox, born 1813.
2. Frances Fox, married John Allen, of Liskeard (*see* page 13)
3. Anna Fox, died *s. p.* at Windermere, 1861, aged 70.
4. Rebecca Phillips Fox, of Kendal, 1872.
(2.) Thomas Fox, of Wellington (see next col).
(3.) Edward Fox, of Gonvena (see page 10).
(4.) Robert Were Fox, died *s. p.* 1753.
(5.) Robert Were Fox, of Kingsbridge (see page 10).
(1.) Mary Fox, married, in 1780, Sylvanus Bevan, of Swansea, and by him, who died July, 1783, had two sons—
  1. Silvanus Bevan, died 10 December, 1819, *s.p.*
  2. Paul Bevan, born 30 August, 1783, married, 24 October, 1804, Rebecca, daughter of Jasper Capper and Ann Fry, his wife, who died 9 November, 1817. He married secondly, 12 May, 1831, Judith Nicholls Dillwyn, born 26 August, 1781, and died 27 June, 1868. He died 12 June, 1868, having had by his 1st wife, five sons and one daughter—
    i. Joseph Bevan, born 10 January, 1807, died 17 August, 1833.
    ii. Sylvanus Bevan, born 8 May, 1808, and died 22 February, 1826.
    iii. Edward Bevan, born 1 November, 1809, married, 11 May, 1850, Maria Goodwin. She was born 14 December, 1818, and died 21 May, 1854. He died 12 April, 1864.
    iv. William Bevan, born 4 October 1812, married, 20 May, 1857, Marie Sofia Read. She was born 25 January, 1835—
      i. John Henry Paul Bevan, born 29 August, 1860.
      i. Antonia Rebecca Bevan, born 5 August, 1862.
      ii. Mary Frances Adelaide Bevan, born 4 Dec., 1863.
      iii. Constance Sofia Bevan, born 25 April, 1865.
      iv. Christine Elsie Bevan, born 20 April, 1867.
    v. Samuel Bevan, born 12 May, 1816, married, 15 August, 1851, Caroline Brooks, born 28 September, 1819, and died 22 October, 1868.
    i. Mary Bevan, born 25 October, 1805, married, 16 July, 1829, to Alfred Waterhouse, who was born 15 June, 1798, and has had five sons and three daughters—
      i. Alfred Waterhouse, born 19 July, 1830, and married, 8 March, 1860, Elizabeth Hodgkin, who was born 16 July, 1834, and has two sons and two daughters—
        1. Paul Waterhouse, born 29 October, 1861.
        2. Alfred Maurice Waterhouse, born 19 April, 1868.
        1. Mary Monica Waterhouse, born 31 Aug., 1863.

        2. Florence Eliot Waterhouse, born 11 November, 1866.
      ii. Theodore Waterhouse, born 12 April, 1838.
      iii. William Waterhouse, born 26 October, 1839, married, 12 April, 1866, Mary Janet Burges, who died 1 October, 1868. He died 1 October, 1869.
      iv. Edwin Waterhouse, born 4 June, 1841, married, 3 April, 1869, Georgina Emma Catherine Thöl, born 30 October, 1848, and has—
        Agnes Mary Waterhouse, born 14 June, 1870.
      v. Sylvanus Bevan Waterhouse, born 11 and died 14 April, 1844.
      i. Ellen Waterhouse, born 14 March, 1832, married, 9 May, 1855, to Wilson, only son of Wilson Crewdson, of Manchester, and his wife Margaret Robson. He was born 9 December, 1832, and has had three sons and two daughters—
        1. Wilson Crewdson, born 13 April, 1856.
        2. Harold Bevan Crewdson, born 28 April, 1861, died 7 November, 1865.
        3. Herbert Cecil Crewdson, born 22 Nov., 1865.
        1. Ethel Mary Crewdson, born 22 Dec. 1859.
        2. ———, daughter, born 28 March, 1872.
      ii. Maria Waterhouse, born 21 February, 1834.
      iii. Katharine Waterhouse, born 20 April, 1836, married, 30 June, 1870, to George Tunstal Redmayne. He was born 27 December, 1840, and has—
        1. Martin Redmayne, born 13 November, 1871.
(2.) Elizabeth Fox, married 1789, to William Matravers, of Westbury, and had five sons and two daughters—
  1. John Matravers, died *s. p.*
  2. William Matravers, married Caroline Howard, of Ipswich, and has had issue five sons and four daughters—
    i. William Matravers, died *s. p.*
    ii. John Howard Matravers, married Mary Evill Overbury, and has a daughter, Marian Howard Matravers.
    iii. Thomas Matravers, married Mary Willoughby Percy, and has two sons and three daughters, viz. *i.* Percy Howard Matravers; *ii.* William Thomas Matravers; *i.* Caroline Alice Maud Matravers; *ii.* Mary Elizabeth Matravers; *iii.* Lucy Mabel Matravers.
    iv. Edward Matravers, married Emma Crawley, and has two sons, viz.: *i.* Ernest Edward Matravers; *ii.* Herbert Henry Matravers.
    v. Henry Matravers.
    i. Elizabeth Howard Matravers, married to Alfred Newton Herapath, and has three sons and three daughters, viz.; *i.* Howard Matravers Herapath; *ii.* Stanley Howard Herapath; *iii.* Alfred Edward Herapath; *i.* Caroline Elizabeth Herapath; *ii.* Constance Maud Herapath; *iii.* Beatrice Mary Herapath.
    ii. Mary Matravers.
    iii. Caroline Matravers, died *s. p.*
    iv. Lucy Matravers, married to Ernest Awdry Stiles.
  3. John Matravers, F.S.A., One of H.M. honourable band of Gentlemen-at-Arms. He was joint owner, with the late William Stiffe, Esq., of the island of Lundy, in 1830-1836; died 30 November, 1851.
  4. Thomas Matravers, died *s. p.*
  1. Elizabeth Matravers, died *s. p.* 1820.
  2. Mary Matravers, died *s. p.*
(3.) Sarah Fox, died *s. p.* 1761.
(4.) Tabitha Fox, married William Cookworthy, *née* Fox, died *s. p.* (see page 11).

FOX, OF WELLINGTON.

THOMAS FOX, of Wellington, 2nd son of Edward Fox, of Wadebridge (see preceding column), married Sarah Smith, and died 1821, having had nine sons and six daughters, viz.—

(1) Thomas Fox, married Catherine Alexander, of Ipswich, and had two sons and three daughters—

1. Thomas Fox, of the Court, Wellington, born 5 February, 1828, married 3rd October, 1855, Sarah Maria, eldest daughter of John Eliot Howard, of Tottenham, and had four sons and five daughters—
   i. Thomas Fox, born 16th March, 1858.
   ii. John Howard Fox, born 8th June, 1864.
   iii. William Alexander Fox, born 28th December, 1865.
   iv. Robert Algernon Fox, born 13th April, 1868.
   i. Catherine Maria, ob. enfans.
   ii. Maria Howard. iii. Eleanor, ob. enfans. iv. Anna Priscilla; and v. Florence Mary Fox.
2. Dykes Alexander Fox, of Birkenhead, unmarried.
1. Catherine Brewster Fox, married to Robert, son of James Charleton, of Bristol, by his first wife, and has an only son, Robert Ash Charleton.
2. Priscilla Fox, died s. p.
3. Anna Fox, married to Frederick Hingston Fox, of Kingsbridge, second son of George Fox, of Ford Park, Plymouth, (see next page).

(2.) Edward Fox, married Hannah Alexander. He died 1845, having had two sons and one daughter—
1. George Smith Fox, of Wellington, married Jane Dobree, and has Edward Carteret Dobree Fox : Jane Hannah Mary Fox; Helen Emily Hankey Fox; Samuel George Dobree Fox.
2. Edward Fox, of the 2nd Somerset Militia, died s. p. 1862.
1. Hannah Alexander Fox, died s. p. 1839.

(3.) George Fox, died s. p. 1811.
(4.) Sylvanus Fox, died s. p.
(5.) Sylvanus Fox, married Mary, daughter of John Sanderson, of London, who died in 1846. He died 1851, having had two sons and five daughters—
1. Sylvanus Fox, J.P., now of Linden, Wellington.
2. Sanderson Fox, died s. p.
1. Mary Fox, 2. Sarah Fox, 3. Margaret Fox, and 4. Elizabeth Fox, all living unmarried, 1872.
5. Anna Rebecca Fox, married Edward Burnett Tylor, F.R.S., of London, now of Wellington.

(6.) Samuel Fox, of Tottenham, married first, Maria Middleton, and had three sons—
1. Benjamin Middleton Fox, died s. p.
2. Samuel Lindoe Fox, married Rachel Elizabeth Fox, eldest daughter of Alfred Fox, of Falmouth (see also page 12). She married 2ndly, Philip D. Tuckett (see page 20). S. L. Fox died in 1862, and left issue—
   i. Samuel Middleton Fox; and Charlotte Maria Fox.
3. Joseph Hoyland Fox, of Wellington, married in 1860 his cousin, Mariana Fox Tuckett (see page 20), of Frenchay, and has had Marion Charlotte Fox, Francis Hugh Fox, Gerald Fox, Margaret Winifred Fox, and Dorothea Elizabeth Fox, who died young.
Samuel Fox married second, 1849, his cousin, Charlotte Fox, of Falmouth (see page 11).

(7.) Henry Fox, died s. p.
(8.) Henry Fox, of Tonedale, Wellington, born 10th March, 1800, married, at Kendal, 6th February, 1833, Rachel, eldest daughter of William Dillworth Crewdson, and has issue—
1. Rachel Crewdson Fox, married, at Wellington, 13th September, 1854, to John Edward, son of Edward William Wakefield, of Kendal, who died at Malvern, 30th July, 1858, leaving issue—
   i. John Edward William Wakefield, born at Ventnor, 31st March, 1858.
   i. Rachel Mary Wakefield.
2. Henrietta Maria Fox, married, at Wellington, 14th March, 1861, to Robert Luke Howard, 2nd son of Robert Howard, of Tottenham, and has issue—
   i. Robert Llewellyn Howard, born 19th August, 1863.

ii. Henry Howard, born 3rd December, 1868.
i. Mary Howard. ii. Rachel Edith Howard. iii. Maria bella Howard.
(9.) Charles Fox, married Sarah Crewdson (see below).
(1.) Sarah Fox, died s. p. 1852.
(2.) Anna Fox, married to John Sanderson, of London, died s. p. 1831.
(3.) Mary Fox, died s. p.
(4.) Elizabeth Fox, died s. p. in 1793.
(5.) Elizabeth Fox, married in 1835 (second wife) to James Charleton, who died 1847, and died s. p. 1867.
(6.) Rebecca Fox, died s. p. 1799.

FOX OF WELLINGTON.

CHARLES FOX, of Wellington, ninth and youngest son of Thomas and Sarah Fox (see above), born 7th April, 1801, married, at Kendal, 13th September, 1827, Sarah, 2nd daughter of William Dillworth Crewdson, and died 5th December, 1860, leaving five sons and one daughter—

1. Dillworth Crewdson Fox, born at Wellington, 11th September, 1828; married, at Wellington, 27th May, 1851, Mary Augusta, daughter of Thomas Woodward Buckham and Mary Cecilia Moore Champ, his wife. She was born at Chelsea, 23rd October, 1827, and has issue—
   i. Charles Dillworth Fox, born at Wellington, 1st March, 1852.
   ii. Henry Fox, born at Wellington, 30th September, 1856.
   iii. Thomas Newland Fox, born at Wellington, 21st June, 1863.
   i. Mary Cecilia Fox, born at Wellington, 13th September, 1853.
   ii. Sarah Anna Fox, born at Wellington, 15th May, 1855.
   iii. Alice Fox, born at Wellington, 20th April, 1858.
   iv. Louisa Fox, born at Wellington, 7th July, 1861.
2. Charles Henry Fox, born at Wellington, 1st April, 1830; died 1831.
3. Dr. Wilson Fox, Physician Ex. to H.M. the Queen, born at Wellington, 2nd November, 1831; married, at Cheltenham, 20th April, 1859, Emily Anne, daughter of Wellesley Doyle, Esq., and Emily Sarah, his wife. She was born at Brompton, 15th April, 1836, and died at Long Ashton, near Bristol, 20th November, 1870, and has issue—
   i. William Arthur Fox, born at Newcastle-under-Lyme, 10th May, 1861.
   ii. Wilson Henry Fox, born in London, 18th August, 1863.
   iii. Francis Sylvanus Wolaston Fox, born at Kendal, 7th July, 1866.
   i. Emily Cecile Fox, born at Newcastle-under-Lyme, 22nd February, 1860.
   ii. Harriett Edith Fox, born in London, 15th February, 1865.
   iii. Adeline Elizabeth Fox, born in London, 17th January, 1870.
4. Charles Henry Fox, born at Wellington, 17th March, 1835; married, at Brighton, 21st October, 1863, Caroline, daughter of John Mellar Chapman. She was born at Usworth, co. Durham, 15th December, 1838, and has issue, all born at Wellington, Somerset—
   i. Charles Leslie Fox, born 24th June, 1865.
   ii. Reginald Wilson Fox, born 1st November, 1866.
   i. Caroline Hilda Macnaughten Fox, born 26th September, 1867.
5. William Francis Fox, born at Wellington, 11th March, 1837; married, at Plymouth, 3rd October, 1862, Charlotte Parker, daughter of Charles (see page 19), by his 2nd wife, Louisa Jane, daughter of Sir William George Parker, Bart. She was born at Plymouth, 8th June, 1841, and died at Nottingham, 13th June, 1872, having had—
   i. William Herbert Fox, born at Nottingham, 7th December, 1863.

i. Charlotte Ethel Fox, born at Nottingham, 27th August, 1865.
ii. Gertrude Louisa Fox, born at Nottingham, 27th September, 1866.
iii. Marion Beatrice Fox, born at Nottingham, 12th July, 1868 ; died 16th May, 1869.
iv. Frances Margaret Fox, born at Nottingham, 12th May, 1870, and died at Plymouth, 27th October, 1870.
v. Ellen Theodora Fox (a twin with Frances Margaret), born at Nottingham, 12th May, 1870.
1. Sarah Anna Fox, born at Wellington, 19th May, 1833.

FOX OF WADEBRIDGE.

EDWARD FOX, of Gonvena, Wadebridge, 3rd son of Edward Fox, of Wadebridge (see page 8), married, 1792, Mary, daughter of John and Mary Brown, of Landrake, Cornwall. He died 1817, having had four sons and three daughters—

(1.) Edward Fox, died s. p. 1793.
(2.) Edward Fox, of Exeter, (born at Gonvena), married, 1820, Johannah Menhennit. He died at Exeter, 1844, having had four sons and eight daughters—

1. Edward Fox, born 1820, not married.
2. George Henry Fox, born 1823, died s. p. 1824.
3. George Henry Fox, died s. p. 1863, at Adelaide, South Australia.
4. Philip Browne Fox, born 1837, married, 1863, at Melbourne, Australia, Helen Patterson, and has Edward Fox, Helen Fox, and Margaret Fox.
1. Mary Anna Fox, born 1821, living at Devonport, 1872.
2. Emma Fox, died s. p. 1823.
3. Emma Fox, married, 1852, Joseph Peirce, of Newport, and has Edwin Peirce, born 1854, Emma Marian Peirce, born 1856, Owen Joseph Peirce, born 1858, William Knox Peirce, born 1862, and Alice Josephine Peirce, born 1865.
4. Catherine Fox, born 1825, married J. Morehead, at Melbourne, no family.
5. Jane Fox, born 1826, died 1828.
6. Charlotte Fox, born 1829, married, 1856, at Kingston-on-Thames, to Joseph James Sessions (deceased), and has William Henry Sessions, born 1857; Joseph James Sessions, born 1859.
7. Sophia Fox, born 1832, married at Melbourne, Australia, Henry B. Foot (deceased), and has Harriet Foot, Charles Foot, born 1855, Emma Foot.
8. Jessie Elizabeth Fox, born 1843, died s. p. 1843.

(3.) George Fox (born at Gonvena, 1799), of Ford Park, Plymouth, married, 1819, at Plymouth, Rachel Collier Hingston, daughter of Joseph Hingston by his second wife, Catherine Phillips Tregelles (see Hingston family, page 19.) He has had nine sons and four daughters, viz.—

1. Edwin Fox, merchant in London, born 1822, married, 1850, Margaret, daughter of —— Wylie, of Devonshire Street, Portland Place, London, and has Edwin Spencer Fox, born 1852; Edith Margaret Fox, Ethel Mary Fox, Jessie Beatrice Fox, Arthur Elliston Fox, born 1862, Mildred Charlotte, born 1867.
2. Frederick Hingston Fox, of Oakhill, Torquay, born 1825, married at Bristol to Anna Fox, daughter of the late Thomas and Catherine Fox, of Wellington and Ipswich, as mentioned on the preceding page.
3. George Edward Fox, merchant at Plymouth, born 1826, married, 1860, Jane Wakefield Richardson, eldest daughter of James Greer and Charlotte Richardson, of Trew-mount Moy, Ireland, and has Edward Fox, born 1861; Harriette Fox, born 1863, Charlotte Wakefield Fox, Walter Richardson Fox, Charles Louis Fox, George Raymond Fox.
4. Pennington Fox, died s. p. 1831.
5. Joseph Hingston Fox, born 1835, married, 1871, Sarah Elizabeth Tregelles.
6. Albert Fox, born 1837, died 1867.
7. Richard Reynolds Fox, born 27 March, 1840 ; married at

Manchester, 3 October, 1867, Frances Elizabeth, younger daughter of Wilson Crewdson, of Manchester.
8. Francis William Fox, of Bristol, born 1841.
9. Charles Alfred Fox, of Plymouth, born 1848.
1. Mary Catherine Fox, died s. p. 1831.
2. Rachel Anna Fox, married at Kingsbridge, 1860, to Henry Bevington Gibbins, of Neath, and has Bevington Henry Gibbins, born 1861; Alfred Gibbins, born 1864; Georgina Mary Gibbins, born 1866; Cecil Gibbins, born 1868; Constance Ethel Gibbins, born 1871.
3. Charlotte Elizabeth Fox, born 1832.
4. Mary Catherine Fox, born 1843.

(4.) Francis Fox, of Elmslea, Tottenham (born at Gonvena, 1797), married Rachel, second daughter of Robert and Jane Womersley. He died 28 January, 1862, leaving one son and one daughter—

1. Francis Edward Fox, born at Tottenham, 28 January, 1834, married at Manchester, 2 September, 1858, Maria, elder daughter of Wilson and Margaret Crewdson, of Manchester, and has had Rachel Maria Fox, born 1859, died 1860; Francis Wilson Fox, born 1860; Albert Fox, died s. p. 1862; William Eustace Fox, died 1864; Margaret Theodora Fox, Helen Mary Fox, Constance Marian Fox, Percy Crewdson Fox, Alfred Francis Hubert Fox.
1. Mary Jane Fox, born 1831, married, March, 1864, her cousin, Alfred Lloyd Fox, of Falmouth (see page 12).

(1.) Mary Fox } both living at Plymouth, 1872.
(2.) Anna Fox }
(3.) Charlotte Fox, died s. p. 1854, aged 51.

ROBERT WERE FOX, 5th son of Edward Fox, of Wadebridge (see page 8), born at Wadebridge, 1758, married at Kingsbridge, 1790, Dorothy, second daughter of John and Rachel Hingston, of Kingsbridge (see page 18). He died 1793, leaving one son and two daughters :—

(1.) Robert Were Fox, of Exeter, born at Wadebridge, 1792, married at Kingsbridge, 1815, Rachel Cookworthy Prideaux, daughter of George and Anna Prideaux, of Kingsbridge (see page 18). He has had ten sons and one daughter—

1. Robert Were Fox, dentist, in Bristol, born 1816, married, 1842, Sarah Sturge, of Bristol, died s. p. 1859.
2. Francis Fox, of Bristol, born, 1818, engineer of the Bristol and Exeter Railway, married, 1848, Charlotte, daughter of William Jackson and Charlotte Monkhouse, and has had issue—Frances Elizabeth Fox, died s. p. 1850; Francis William Fox, born 1851; Robert Henry Fox, died s. p. 1855; Charles Prideaux Fox, born 1855; Anna Mary Fox, died s. p. 1864; Charlotte Elizabeth Fox, born 1859; Florence Monkhouse Fox, born 1860.
3. Charles Prideaux Fox, born 1820, a Roman Catholic priest.
4. George Frederic Fox born 1822, a dentist at Gloucester, married at Waterford, 1 August, 1850, Sarah Anne, daughter of Joshua and Isabella Newsom, and has had issue Frederick Newsom Fox, died s. p. 1863; Isabella Fox, born 1852; Walter Henry Fox, born 1854; George Prideaux Fox, died s. p. 1860; Robert Fox, born 1857; Ernest William Fox, born 1859; Charles Herbert Fox, born 1861; Annie Prideaux Fox, born 1863; Freda Mary Fox, born 1865; George Frederic Fox, born 1867; Ethel Charlotte Fox, born 1868; and Dora Evelyn Fox, born 1869.
5. William Cookworthy Fox, died s. p. at Bristol, 1824.
6. Sylvanus Bevan Fox, born 1825, a dentist at Exeter.
7. William Henry Fox, died s. p. at Exeter, 1832.
8. Octavius Annesley Fox, born 1829, a dentist at Brighton, married there 20th September, 1865, Miriam, daughter of John and Mary Simmonds, and has two daughters, Anna Mary Fox, born 1866; and Alice Miriam Fox, born 1869.
9. John Hingston Fox, born 1830, a civil engineer, now of Bristol, married at Bristol, 1860, Frances, daughter of William Jackson and Charlotte Monkhouse, and has issue Ellen Mary Fox, born 1861; Catherine Prideaux Fox, born 1862; William Hingston Fox, born 1863, died 1870; John Herbert Fox, born 1865; Walter Collier Fox, born 1866;

Frances Marion Fox, died young; Philip Henry Fox, born 1870; and Emily Charlotte Fox, a twin with Margaret Ethel Fox, born 1871.

10. Walter Henry Fox, died *s. p.* at Exeter, 1835.

1. Rachel Prideaux Fox, born 1817.

(1.) Dorothy Fox, born 1791.

(2.) Rachel Anna Fox, born at Wadebridge, 1794, died *s. p.* 1798.

FOX OF PAR.

GEORGE FOX, of Par (see also page 6), married second, in 1726, Anna, daughter of Philip Debell, of East Looe, and Anna Soady, his wife (see page 19), and by her had three sons and five daughters—

(1.) George Croker Fox, of Falmouth, ancestor of Fox of Grove Hill, Falmouth, Plymouth, &c. (see below).

(2.) Joseph Fox, of Falmouth (of whom see page 12).

(3.) Francis Fox, of Plymouth, born 1736, married, 1760, Sarah, daughter of William Cookworthy, well known as a chemist and as the discoverer of Kaolin in Cornwall, which led to the manufacture of china in England (see page 18), and died 1769, having had two sons and one daughter—

1. William Fox (changed his name to Cookworthy), married, 1st, Tabitha Fox, daughter of Edward Fox, of Wadebridge, and his wife, Anna Were, who died *s. p.* (see page 8); he married, second, Elizabeth Howard, died *s. p.*

2. Francis Fox, married, 1798, Sarah, only daughter of John Birkbeck, of Settle, and his wife Sarah Wilson, and had issue—Francis William Fox, who died in infancy, and Sarah Fox, married to William Dillworth Crewdson, Esq., of Helme Lodge, Kendal.

1. Sarah Fox, died *s. p.*

(1.) Tabitha Fox, died *s. p.* 1801, aged 70.

(2.) Mary Fox, died *s. p.*

(3.) Sarah Fox, married in 1757, Joel Cadbury, of Exeter, and had two children; viz.—

1. John Cadbury, married Anna ——.

2. Anna Cadbury, married Samuel Churchill, of Exeter, and had six sons and three daughters—

i. Samuel Churchill, married Anne Buckingham.

ii. John Churchill, married ——.

iii. Joel Churchill. iv. George Fox Churchill. v. James Churchill. vi. Charles Churchill.

i. Anna Churchill, married ——.

ii. Maria Churchill, married to Pearson Allen, and had Richard Pearson Allen.

iii. Sarah Tabitha Churchill.

(4) Anna Fox, died *s. p.* 1757, aged 20.

(5.) Rachel Fox, married, 1760, to John Hingston (see page 18), and had issue—

1. Rachel Hingston, died *s. p.* 1762.

FOX OF GROVE HILL.

GEORGE CROKER FOX, of Falmouth (eldest son of George Fox, of Par, and his second wife, Anna Debell, (see above), married, 1749, Mary, third daughter of Thomas Were, of Wellington, county Somerset, and by her had issue six sons and three daughters—

(1.) George Croker Fox, of Grove Hill, Falmouth, married Catherine, daughter and co-heir of William Young, of Leominster, and niece of James Payton, Esq., of Dudley. He died 1807, leaving—

1. George Croker Fox, of Grove Hill, married, 1810, Lucy, daughter of the late Robert Barclay, Esq., of Bury Hill, Surrey, but dying 1850, without issue, left Grove Hill to Robert Barclay Fox, only son of his first cousin, Robert Were Fox, of Falmouth. Mrs. G. C. Fox died February, 1859.

1. Catherine Payton Fox, died 1823 *s. p.*

(2.) Robert Were Fox, of Falmouth, married Elizabeth, daughter of Joseph Tregelles, of Falmouth, and Sarah Hingston, his wife (see page 19), and by her had seven sons and three daughters—

1. Robert Were Fox, F.R.S., of Penjerrick, married, 1812, Maria, daughter of Robert Barclay, Esq., of Bury Hill, Surrey; and by her, who died 1858, he had one son and two daughters—

i. Robert Barclay Fox, married, 1844, Jane Gurney Backhouse, and died at Cairo, 1855. She died at Pau, in 1860, leaving

i. Robert Fox, now of Grove Hill; born 1845, married, 1867, Ellen Mary, daughter of Francis and Ellen Bassett, of the Heath, Leighton, Bedford, and has a daughter—
Lilian Isabel Fox, born 1868.

ii. George Croker Fox, born 1847, married, 1871, Ada Mary, daughter of Baldwin Arden Wake, Captain R.N., and has a son -
George Croker Fox, born 1871.

iii. Henry Backhouse Fox.

iv. Joseph Gurney Fox.

i. Jane Hannah Backhouse Fox.

i. Anna Maria Fox.

ii. Caroline Fox, died 1871 *s. p.*, aged 51.

2. George Philip Fox, died *s. p.*

3. Joshua Fox, of Tregedna, married Joanna Flannering, and had three daughters—

i. Josephine Fox, married to James Bull, Commander R.N.

ii. Marie Louise Fox. iii. Joanna Ellen Fox, married Rev. — Davis.

4. Alfred Fox, of Glen Dourgan and Falmouth, married Sarah, daughter of Samuel Lloyd, of Bordesley, in Warwickshire, and by her had twelve children (see next page).

5. Henry Francis Fox, died *s. p.* 1809.

6. Charles Fox, of Trebah, married Sarah Hustler, of Ulverston, and by her had two daughters—

i. Juliet Mary Fox, married to Edmund Backhouse, M.P. of Darlington, and has 1. Jonathan Edmund Backhouse, who married 29th November, 1871, Florence, daughter of Sir John Salusbury Trelawny, Bart., M.P., of Trelawne, Cornwall; 2. Charles Hubert Backhouse; 1. Sarah Juliet Backhouse; 2. Millicent Evelyn Backhouse.

ii. Jane Catherine Fox, died *s. p.* 1833.

7. Louis Fox, died *s. p.* 1840.

1. Charlotte Fox, married to her cousin, Samuel Fox, of Tottenham (see page 9), now of Falmouth.

2. Elizabeth Tregelles Fox, married to William Gibbins, died *s. p.* 1837.

3. Mariana Fox, married to Francis Tuckett (see page 20).

(3.) Philip Fox, died *s. p.* 1775, aged 20.

(4.) William Were Fox, died *s. p.* 1775, aged 16.

(5.) Joshua Fox, died *s. p.* 1791, aged 31.

(6.) Thomas Were Fox, of Falmouth, married, 1792, Mary, daughter of Joseph Tregelles and Sarah Hingston his wife (see p. 19), and died 1844, aged 78, having had four sons; viz.—

1. Thomas Were Fox, of Plymouth, born April, 1793, married, 1814, Eliza Grigg, who died in 1862. He died 1860, having had nine sons and four daughters, viz.—

i. Thomas Were Fox, of Plymouth, merchant, &c., born 1817, married Frances Mary Hole, and died in 1870, leaving issue Frances Adeline Fox; Thomas Were Fox, born 1855; Blanche Fox; Arthur Hole Fox and George Croker Fox, twins, born 1858; Alice Maud Fox; Florence Fox; Amy Fox and Walter Grigg Fox, born 1864.

ii. Henry Fox, of Plymouth, merchant, &c., born 1819, married Mary Charlotte Russell, and has issue William Russell Fox, born 1846; Mary Kate Fox; Eliza Frances Fox; Henry Elliott Fox, died *s. p.*; Frederick Henry Fox, died *s. p.*; Percival Bradshaw Fox, born 1859; Edward Lawrence Fox, born 1861, and Frederick Russell Fox, born 1864.

[11]

iii. George Croker Fox, died *s. p.* 1834.
iv. Charles James Fox, born 1823, married Amelia Pitt, and died 1859, leaving Charles James Pitt Fox, born 1853.
v. Philip Fox (in Canada), born 1824, married Isabella Ormiston, and has issue Lydia Ormiston Fox, who died 1864; William Andrew Fox, born 1858; Eliza Jane Fox; Janet Fox; Mary Charlotte Fox; Alfred Hingston Fox, born 1865; Isabella Fox and Florence Fox.
vi. Arthur Fox, born 1826.
vii. Septimus Fox, died *s. p.* 1863.
viii. Octavius Fox, died *s. p.*
ix. William Frederick Fox, died *s. p.*
i. Eliza Mary Fox, died *s. p.* 1830.
ii. Jane Fox, died *s. p.* 1817.
iii. Adeline Fox, married to Rev. Edward Wilson Cooke, M.A., and has issue Adeline Longueville Cooke; Emily Tregelles Cooke; Foxcrowle Percival Cooke, born 1861; Archibald Stevington Cooke, born 1864.
iv. Eliza Mary Jane Fox, married to William Henry Charsley, of Oxford.
2. William Fox, died *s. p.*
3. William Fox, of Gloucester, married first, Elizabeth Windeatt, who died 1838, having had—
i. William Fox, died *s. p.* i. Mary Elizabeth Fox, born 1834.
He married second, 1844, Elizabeth Cosserat, and died in 1866, leaving—
i. William Fox, born 1847. i. Frances Fox.
4. Frederic Fox, died *s. p.* 1830.
(1.) Mary Fox, of Penjerrick, died *s. p.* 1839, aged 89.
(2.) Anna Fox, died *s. p.* 1809, aged 52.
(3.) Charlotte Fox, died *s. p.* 1785, aged 23.

FOX OF FALMOUTH.

ALFRED FOX, of Glen Dourgan, and Falmouth, 4th son of Robert Were Fox, of Falmouth (see preceding page), born 9th September, 1794, married, at Birmingham, 15th May, 1828, Sarah, youngest daughter of Samuel and Rachel Lloyd, of Birmingham, and has had six sons and six daughters—
(1.) Alfred Lloyd Fox, born at Falmouth, 26th May, 1829; married, at Tottenham, 15th March, 1864, Mary Jane, daughter of Francis Fox, of Tottenham (see page 10), and has issue—
1. Alfred Francis Fox, born at Penmere, Falmouth, 7th April, 1867.
2. Hubert Fox, born 15th January, 1870.
(2.) Theodore Fox, born at Falmouth, 4th April, 1831; married, at Norwich, 26th March, 1857, Harriet Howell, daughter of John Paul Kirkbride, and Ann Eliza his wife. She was born at Bristol, 14th January, 1828, and has issue—
1. Theodore Alfred Fox, born at Drymma, near Neath, 1st February, 1858.
2. Edwin Kirkbride Fox, born at Drymma, near Neath, 14th May, 1859.
3. Herbert Lloyd Fox, born at Drymma, near Neath, 29th June, 1863.
1. Eliza Gurney Fox, born at Drymma, near Neath, 9th July, 1861.
2. Harriet Beatrice Fox, born at Pinchinthorpe, Guisboro', 30th September, 1865.
(3.) Howard Fox, born at Falmouth, 10th December, 1836; married, at St. John's Wood, London, 19th March, 1864, Olivia Blanche, daughter of Charles and Eliza Orme, of Avenue Road, London, and has issue, all born at Falmouth—
1. Howard Orme Fox, born 16th August, 1865.
2. Charles Masson Fox, born 9th November, 1866.
1. Olivia Lloyd Fox, born 5th February, 1868.
(4.) Charles William Fox, born at Falmouth, 13th June, 1843; died at Neath Abbey, 18th June, 1866.
(5.) George Henry Fox, born at Falmouth, 27th September, 1845.

(6.) Wilson Lloyd Fox, born at Falmouth, 27th January, 1847.
(1.) Rachel Elizabeth Fox, born at Falmouth, 6th February, 1833; married, 1st, at Falmouth, 27th April, 1854, to Samuel Lindoe, son of Samuel and Maria Fox (see page 9). He was born at Wellington, 6th June, 1830; died at Tottenham, 22nd November, 1862, and left issue—
1. Samuel Middleton Fox, born at Tottenham, 16th March, 1856.
1. Charlotte Maria Fox, born at Tottenham, 23rd December, 1857.
Rachel Elizabeth Fox, married, 2ndly, at Falmouth, 11th September, 1867, Philip Debell Tuckett, son of P. D. Tuckett, of Frenchay (see page 20), and has issue—
1. Philip Debell Tuckett, born in London, 22nd December, 1868.
2. Percival Fox Tuckett, born in London, 21st August, 1870.
(2.) Sarah Charlotte Fox, married, at Falmouth, 27th October, 1852, to Robert Nicholas Fowler, Esq., M.P. for Penrhyn, M.A. and J.P., only son of Thomas Fowler, Esq. He was born at Tottenham, 12th September, 1828, and has had issue, one son and nine daughters—
1. Thomas Fowler, born in London, 12th August, 1868.
1. Lucy Charlotte; 2. Charlotte Rachel; 3. Helen Ann; 4. Mary; 5. Harriet Mary, died young; 6. Caroline; 7. Jean Elizabeth; 8. Octavia Louisa; and 9. Bertha Sophia Fowler.
(3.) Mary Fox, married, at Falmouth, 24th August, 1854, to Joseph Whitwell Pease, Esq., M.P. for South Durham since 1865, and a magistrate for co. Durham and North Riding of Yorkshire, and has issue—
1. Alfred Edward Pease, born 29th June, 1857.
2. Joseph Albert Pease, born 17th January, 1860.
1. Emma Josephine. 2. Sarah Charlotte. 3. Maud Mary. 4. Helen Blanche. 5. Lucy Ethel; and 6. Agnes Claudia Fox Pease.
(4.) Helen Maria Fox, born at Falmouth, 17th November, 1838; married, at Falmouth, 13th September, 1860, John William, son of John Beaumont Pease. He was born at Darlington, 13th August, 1836, and has issue—
1. Howard Pease, born at Saltwell, Gateshead, 12th July, 1863.
2. John William Beaumont Pease, born at Pendower, Newcastle-upon-Tyne, 4th July, 1869.
1. Sarah Helen Pease, born at Gateshead, 17th July, 1861.
2. Alice Pease, born at Saltwell, 23rd October, 1865, and died there, 29th August, 1867.
3. Florence Pease, born at Pendower, 8th September, 1867.
(5.) Lucy Anna Fox, born at Falmouth, 5th October, 1841; married, at Falmouth, 7th August, 1861, Thomas, son of John and Elizabeth Hodgkin. He was born at Tottenham, 29th July, 1831, and has issue—
1. John Alfred Hodgkin, born at Benwell Dene, 27th February, 1871, and died 5th February, 1872.
1. Lucy Violet Hodgkin, born at Benwell Dene, near Newcastle-upon-Tyne, 19th March, 1869.
(6.) Sophia Lloyd Fox, born at Falmouth, 28th September, 1848, and died 1870, unmarried.

FOX OF FALMOUTH.

JOSEPH FOX,* of Falmouth, a surgeon, 2nd son of George Fox, of Par, by his second marriage (see page 11), married, 1754, Elizabeth, daughter of Richard Hingston, Surgeon, of Penryn, and had issue six sons and five daughters—
(1.) Joseph Fox, M.D., of London, afterwards of Wood Cottage, Mylor, near Falmouth, physician for many years to the London

---

* In some circumstances which occurred during the American war, the disinterested conduct of Mr. Joseph Fox, surgeon, of Falmouth, deserves to be recorded as exhibiting a striking instance of attachment to the principles of peace, and of a resolution not to participate in profits derived through war. Mr. Fox had a small share in two cutters, with other owners, who, at the

Hospital, married Elizabeth, daughter of Charles Peters and Anna Tregelles (see page 19), but there was not any issue of the marriage. He died at Plymouth, February, 1832.

(2.) Edward Long Fox, M.D., of Brislington House, near Bristol, ancestor of a numerous family: for them see next page, under *Fox of Brislington.*

(3.) Richard Fox, M.D., of Falmouth, born 1764, married, 1786, Hannah, daughter of Josiah Forster, of St. Paul's Churchyard, London. He died at Falmouth, 1841, having had by her three sons and two daughters—

1. Richard Hingston Fox, born 1787, Surgeon, Falmouth, died *s. p.* 1818.
2. Josiah Forster Fox, born 1788.
3. Joseph Fox, Surgeon at Falmouth, born 1792, married, 1819, Anna Peters, daughter of Samuel Tregelles, of Falmouth, and his wife, Rebecca Smith (see page 19), and died 1861, having had by her nine sons and four daughters—
   i. Joseph John Fox, Surgeon at Stoke Newington, born 1821, married 1847, Sarah Angell, daughter of Charles Allen, of Coggeshall, Essex, and has had Hugh Courtenay Fox, Surgeon, born 1848; Charles Allen Fox, born 1849; Joseph John Fox, born 1852; Richard Hingston Fox, born 1853; Joseph Tregelles Fox, born 1855; John Raleigh Fox, died 1858; Robert Fortescue Fox, born 1858; Samuel Harris Fox, born 1860; Lydia Forster Fox, born 1863, died 1865.
   ii. Richard Fox, born 1824, died 1825.
   iii. Henry Tregelles Fox, Surgeon at Beechworth, Victoria (Australia), born 1826, married Melita Abrahams, and has had four sons and two daughters, viz.—
      i. Henry Tregelles Fox, born 1863, and died 1870; ii. Marshall Fox, born 1865; iii. John Raymond Fox, born 1867; iv. Charles Alexander Fox, born 1870; i. Alice Elizabeth Fox, born 1859; ii. Josephine Fox, born 1861.
   iv. Richard Francis Fox, born 1827, died *s. p.* 1844.
   v. Samuel Tregelles Fox, born 1830, Surgeon at Falmouth, died *s. p.* 1860.

vi. Edward Joseph Fox, born 1834, twin with Ellen Elizabeth Fox, died *s. p.* 1840.
vii. Nathaniel Fox, of Falmouth, born 1835, married, 1857, Elizabeth, daughter of James B. Cox, of Falmouth, and has issue two sons and six daughters, viz.—
   i. Francis Joseph Fox, born 1859; ii. Arthur Edward Fox, born 1864; i. Anna Elizabeth Fox, born 1858; ii. Ellen Mary Fox, born 1861; iii. Rachel Tregelles Fox, born 1863; iv. Harriet Fox, born 1867; v. Gertrude Fox; vi. Catherine Marshall Fox.
viii. Alexander Fox, Surgeon at Shortlands, near Auckland, New Zealand, born 1837, married, 1869, Ellen, daughter of John Phillips, of Tottenham, and has a daughter, Marian Fox, born 1870.
ix. Edward Marshall Fox, born 1840, died *s. p.* 1866, a chemist at Liverpool.
   i. Anna Priscilla Fox, born 1820, died *s. p.* 1850.
   ii. Rebecca Smith Fox, born 1823.
   iii. Catherine Mary Fox, born 1832, died 1832.
   iv. Ellen Elizabeth Fox, born 1834, twin with Edward Joseph Fox, died 1834.
1. Priscilla Fox, born 1789, died 1800.
2. Elizabeth Fox, born 1791, died 1794.

(4.) Nathaniel Fox, died *s. p.* 1786.
(5.) Francis Fox, married Hester Mills, died *s. p.* 1795.
(6.) Philip Fox, died *s. p.* 1772.
(1.) Anna Fox, married first, to William Rawes; second, to Thomas Thompson, died *s. p.*
(2.) Elizabeth Fox, married, 1784, to John Allen, of Liskeard, and had two children, viz.—
   1. John Allen, of Liskeard, married first, 1812, Frances daughter of George Fox, of Perran, and his wife, Frances James (see page 8), and by her had
      i. John Allen, died *s. p.* 1814.
      i. Frances Allen (who compiled, in 1840, the chart referred to in the Introduction), married in 1847 to Nathaniel Tregelles, and has Frances Elizabeth Tregelles, John Allen Tregelles, Henry Tregeles, Mary Catherine Tregelles, George Fox Tregelles.
   John Allen, married second, 1820, Elizabeth Wright, of Bristol, and died 1859, having had one son and four daughters—
      ii. John Allen, died *s. p.* 1822.
      ii. Mary Allen.
      iii. Elizabeth Allen, married, in 1851, to William Southall, and died 1851 *s. p.*
      iv. Rebecca Allen, married, in 1861, to William Matthews, and has issue John William Matthews, Eliza Jane Matthews, and Rebecca Allen Matthews.
      v. Louisa Allen.
   1. Mary Allen, married, 1811, to John Eliott, and has three sons and three daughters—
      i. John Eliott, of Liskeard, married, in 1859, Mary Ann Sturge, and has Ann Sturge Eliott, born 1860.
      ii. Samuel Eliott, of Plymouth, married, 1843, Jane, daughter of Thomas Mann, of Truro, and has Joseph Eliott, born 1844, who married, in 1870, Alice, daughter of Francis J. Thompson, of Bridgnorth, and has Joseph Thompson Eliott, born 1871; Samuel Eliott, died *s. p.* 1851; John Eliott, died *s. p.*; Thomas Eliott, born 1859; and Sarah Jane Eliott, born 1846; Elizabeth Eliott, born 1848; Mary Anna Eliott, born 1853, died 1859; Caroline Eliott, born 1857, and Gertrude Eliott, born 1862.
      iii. Joseph Eliott, died *s. p.* 1841.
      i. Elizabeth Eliott, born 1812, married, 1853, to Silvanus James, of Truro, who died 1867. She died 1866 *s. p.*
      ii. Mary Eliott.
      iii. Anna Eliott, died *s. p.* 1817.

(3.) Sarah Fox. (4.) Tabitha Fox, and (5.) Rachel Fox, who all died *s. p.*

---

commencement of hostilities with France, in 1778, armed these vessels as letters of marque, in order to capture French merchantmen. He remonstrated against this proceeding, and offered to sell his share, but in vain. The enterprise was successful, and some valuable ships were taken. His partners then endeavoured to prevent him from receiving his share of the profits; but he insisted upon it, and lodged the amount in the British Funds, not disclosing the circumstance to any of his family, but resolving, on the first opportunity, to make full restitution to the French proprietors. On peace being restored, in 1783, he took measures for that purpose, and in 1784 commissioned his son, Dr. Edward Long Fox, to proceed to Paris, where he first communicated the circumstances to him by letter. Much difficulty and delay obstructed the settlement of the business, and early in 1785, while it was yet in progress, Mr. Joseph Fox died. A notice was inserted in the *Gazette de France* of the 25th of February of that year, and applications in consequence being speedily made by most of the sufferers, an amount of about £1470 was restored to the principal claimants, who made an acknowledgment in the same Gazette of August, 1785, as follows:—"L'avis du docteur Anglais Edward Long Fox. "aux personnes intéressés comme propriétaires ou assureurs dans quelques "bâtimens pris dans la derniere guerre, publié dans la Gazette, du 25 Fevrier "dernier, n'a pas été sans effet; les Sieurs Etie, Lefebvre frères de Rouen, "et Martel père du Havre, viennent d'écrire que le docteur Edward Long "Fox a satisfait à leur égard à ce qu'il avoit fait annoncer. C'est conforme-"ment à leur vœu, que l'on donne ici la publicité qu'il merite à ce trait de "générosité et du équité qui honore la société des Quakers et prouve leur "attachement aux principes de paix et d'union qui les caractérisent." A small sum still remained in the hands of Dr. E. L. Fox, the equitable proprietors of which could not be discovered, and the breaking out of the Revolutionary War, and other circumstances, prevented the disposal of it for many years. At length, in 1818, the sum having accumulated by interest to £600, Dr. Fox again proceeded to Paris, and after instituting various inquiries as to the best means of its appropriation, he placed the amount in the treasury of the Invalid Seamen of France, for the relief of non-combatants of the merchant service, the family of Lefebvre, of Rouen, being invested with a limited power to recommend suitable objects. Thus, as far as circumstances would permit, was the original design of the principal agent completely fulfilled. To the honour of the French character it must be stated, that no claim was made by any individual which was not subsequently proved by the documents to be correct. The public advertisement issued by Dr. Fox drew forth an address to him from a body of Protestants in the South of France—viz, at Nismes, Congenies, &c.,—whose religious principles closely resemble those of the Society of Friends.—*Taken chiefly from Burke's "History of the Commoners."*

FOX OF BRISLINGTON.

EDWARD LONG FOX [M.D. of Edinburgh, Member of the "Royal Medical" Society, Edinburgh], of Queen Square, Bristol, and afterwards of Brislington * House, near Bristol, for many years in extensive practice in Bristol, and Physician to the Bristol Royal Infirmary (second son of Joseph Fox, surgeon, of Falmouth, and Elizabeth Hingston, see preceding page), married twice. He married, first, 1784, Catherine Brown, daughter of Edward Brown, Esq., of Wallcott, in the county of Lincoln, who died in London, 23 September, 1803, and was buried at the Foundling Chapel, Brunswick Square, London, and by her had two sons and five daughters, viz.—

(1.) Edward Long Fox, of London, died *s. p.*

(2.) Henry Hawes Fox [M.D., Member and President of the "Royal Medical" Society, Edinburgh], of Berkeley Square, Bristol, and latterly of Northwoods, Gloucestershire, for many years in large practice in Bristol, and Physician to the Bristol Royal Infirmary; married Harriet Jones, and died 1851. Dr. and Mrs. Fox are buried in Brislington Church. They had five children, viz.—

  1. Henry Hawes Fox, of London, married Elizabeth, daughter of —— Gilbert, Esq.

  2. Edward Fox, died *s. p.*

  3. William Charles Fox, Rev., M.B., of the Grange, Frampton-Cotterell,† Gloucestershire, married, first, Eliza Frances, second daughter of the late Rev. George Hunt, of Buckhurst, Berks; she died January, 1861, leaving one daughter—

    i. Alice Mary Fox, born 1859.

  The Rev. William Charles Fox married secondly, August, 1863, Georgina Sarah, eldest daughter of the late Rev. H. Wodehouse, Vicar of Worle, Somerset, and by her has—

    i. Lionel Wodehouse Fox, born 1865.

    ii. Armine Wodehouse Fox, born 1869.

    ii. Eliza Frances Fox, born 1864.

  4. Richard Vaughan Fox, died *s. p.* 1822.

  1. Harriett Charlotte Fox, died *s. p.* 1826.

(1.) Mary Brown Fox, married Charles Louis Muller, of London, and died 1863, aged 76, leaving—

  1. Catherine Fox Muller.

  2. Louisa Hawes Muller.

(2.) Catherine Brown Fox, died *s. p.*

(3.) Anne Fox, died *s. p.*

(4.) Jane Brown Fox, married Henry Davis, Esq. (nephew of the late R. Hart Davis, Esq., formerly M.P. for Bristol), and had issue three sons and three daughters, viz.—

  1. Henry Long Davis, died *s. p.*

  2. Henry Davis.

  3. Edward Long Davis.

  1. Clementina Davis, died *s. p.*

  2. Catherine Davis.

  3. Maria Davis, married in 1866 to —— Motte, Esq., of Grenoble.

(5.) Emma Fox, died *s. p.*

Dr. Edward Long Fox, of Brislington House, married, secondly, in 1805, Isabella Ker, eldest daughter of Major John Charles Ker, of the family of Ker, of Blackshiels, near Edinburgh. He died May 2, 1835, aged 74. She died April 10, 1861, aged 81. Dr. and Mrs. Fox are buried in one grave in the family burial ground, Brislington. They had issue by such marriage, six sons and seven daughters, viz.—

(3.) Charles Joseph Fox, M.D. Cantab., formerly of Brislington House, and of the Beeches, Brislington, and latterly of Fairholme, Torquay, born 21 January, 1806, married at Cheltenham, 1834,

Ellen, youngest daughter and co-heiress of Thomas Lucas, Esq., of London, and Jemima (daughter of Archbishop Newcome, Primate of Ireland) his wife. Mrs. C. Fox died at the Beeches, December, 1855, and Dr. Fox at the Rev. G. L. Cartwright's, Brislington, June, 1870, in his 65th year. Dr. and Mrs. C. Fox are buried in a vault in Arnos Vale Cemetery. They had three sons and seven daughters, viz.—

  1. *Charles Edward Fox, barrister-at-law, born 7 June, 1837. Master and Registrar in Equity, Commissioner for taking Accounts, &c., High Court, Bombay.

  2. Stephen Newcome Fox, born 1849.

  3. Walter Dowell Fox, died *s. p.* 1853.

  1. Ellen Jemima Fox.

  2. Agnes Anna Maria Fox.

  3. Constance Catherine Fox, married at the British Legation, Berne, 3 July, 1867, to Charles Henry Tawney, M.A., late Fellow of Trinity College, Cambridge, and has issue—

    i. Charles Joseph Tawney, born July, 1869.

    i. Constance Ellen Tawney.

    ii. Agnes Susan Tawney.

  4. Annie Newcome Fox.

  5. Edith Fox.

  6. Gertrude Emily Fox.

  7. Madeleine Fox.

(4.) Edwin Fydell Fox, born 6 April, 1807, died *s. p.*

(5.) William Edward Fox, of Clifton, born 30 May, 1811, married in London, 1849, Emma, widow of Sir George Molyneux, Bart., of Castle Dillon, county of Armagh, and has issue three sons and one daughter—

  1. William Edward Ker Fox, born 1850.

  2. John Charles Ker Fox, born 1851.

  3. James Ireland Fox, born 1852.

  1. Isabella Anna Maria Fox

(6.) Edwin Fydell Fox, M.R.C.S., of Kensington Place, Brislington, born 20 April, 1814, married twice. He married first, at Brockley, 1841, Elizabeth Augusta, third daughter of John Hugh Smyth Pigott, Esq., of Brockley, Somerset, and by her, who died June, 1850, and was buried in the churchyard at Brockley, has had issue two sons and three daughters—

  1. Edwin Churchill Pigott Fox, M.B. and C.M. Edinburgh University, born 1842.

  2. Arthur Edward Wellington Fox, M.B. and C.M. Edinburgh University, born 1844; settled at Bath, physician to the Bath Dispensary.

  1. Elizabeth Isabella Louisa Fox, died *s. p.* 1846.

  2. Agnes Catherine Pigott Fox.

  3. Elizabeth Augusta Pigott Fox.

Mr. Edwin Fydell Fox married secondly, July, 1868, at the parish church, Keynsham, Ellen Elizabeth, youngest daughter of William Warrington, Esq., of London, and by her has—

  4. Evelyn Maude Warrington Fox.

(7.) George Frederick Fox, of Keynsham, Somerset (a solicitor in Bristol), born 24 May, 1817; married at Brislington, 1840, Ellin, youngest daughter of the Rev. Thomas Brown Simpson (Vicar of Keynsham, and afterwards of Congresbury, Somerset), and by her has issue two sons and three daughters—

  1. Harry Croker Fox, Royal Engineers, born 1842.

  2. George Gerald Fox, born 1852.

  1. Isabella Ellin Fox, died *s. p.* 1843.

  2. Isabella Maria Fox.

  3. Madelina Helen Fox.

(8.) Washington Fox, formerly of Brislington, afterwards settled in Canada, born 13 January, 1824; married, May, 1860, Mary Desmond Coffin, and died at Niagara, Canada West, October, 1866, leaving—

---

* Brislington is a parish in the County of Somerset, two and a half miles south-east of Bristol, on the high-road to Bath; 2960 acres. Population (at the census of 1861) 1489. Brislington House is a private Asylum for insane persons, three miles from Bristol, erected by Dr. Edward Long Fox in 1806.

† Frampton-Cotterell is a parish in Gloucestershire, four miles west-south-west of Chipping Sodbury. Population 1931. Northwoods is a private asylum for insane persons, erected by the late Dr. Henry Hawes Fox and since his decease, 1851, conducted by Dr. J. G. Davey.

---

* Mr. Charles Edward Fox, in right of his mother, quarters the following arms, viz.:—

Lucas. Argent, on a Canton, Sable, a Ducal Coronet, or.

Knight. Paly, Argent and Gules, on a Canton of the first, a Spur with the Rowel downwards, leathered, or.

De Neufville Azure, a Saltier, or, between four Castles of the same, an Anchor of the first.

1. Arthur Copley Fox, born June, 1864.

(6.) Elizabeth Anne Fox, married to William Goodeve, of Clifton (surgeon), and died 1829, having had one daughter, viz.—
Bettana Goodeve, died *s. p.*

(7.) Madelina Ker Fox.

(8.) Anna Mary Fox, married at Brislington, 1844, to Rev. George Leopold Cartwright, Curate of Brislington, and has issue—
    1. Frederick Fox Cartwright, a solicitor in Bristol, born 1845; married his cousin, Katherine Long Fox Danger, April 13, 1871 (see below) and has issue—
        i. Thomas Cartwright, born 24 May, 1872.
    2. George Edward Sheward Cartwright, 83rd Reg., born 1847
    1. Isabella Mary Louisa Cartwright.

(9.) Emma Selina Fox, died *s. p.* 1862, and is buried in the family burial ground, Brislington.

(10.) Katherine Long Fox, married at Brislington, 1845, to Thomas Danger, Esq., a solicitor in Bristol, and died 1854, and was buried in Arnos Vale Cemetery, having had—
    1. Catherine Louisa Danger, died *s. p.*
    2. Isabel Anne Danger.
    3. Katherine Long Fox Danger, married at Brislington to her cousin, F. F. Cartwright, April 13, 1871 (see above).

(11.) Fanny Sophia Fox, died *s. p.*

(12.) Louisa Caroline Fox, married at Neufchâtel, Switzerland, 1856, to Thomas Danger, Esq., and has issue one son and three daughters—
    1. Louis Charles Danger, born 1860.
    1. Rose Katherine.
    2. Marion Louisa.
    3. Annie Danger.

FOX OF PLYMOUTH.

JOHN FOX, of Plymouth, eldest son of John Fox (see page 7), married, 1747, Rebecca Steevens, of High Wycombe, and had eight sons and four daughters—

(1.) Charles Fox, a chemist, of Falmouth, married Hannah Ferrier, sister to the late Admiral Ferrier, and died in 1811, *s. p.*

(2.) John Fox, d. 1833, aged 80, unm. (3.) Henry Fox, d. 1827, unm.

(4.) Lovall Fox, died 1814, unm. (5.) Josiah Fox, died *s. p.* 1760.

(6.) Spicer Fox, died 1796, unmarried.

(7.) Josiah Fox, married at Philadelphia Anna Miller, and settled in the State of Ohio, North America, and died in 1847, aged 84, having had four sons and four daughters—
    1. John Fox, *ob. enf.*   2. John Charles Fox, *ob. enf.*
    3. Charles James Fox, born October, 1805, married, 7 February, 1837, Esther Cooper, and has issue—
        i. William Spicer Fox, born 22 September, 1839.
        ii. Francis Cooper Fox, born 1 November, 1855.
        i. Anna Miller Fox, born 2 May, 1838.
        ii. Sarah Cooper Fox, born 14 November, 1841.
    4. Francis Drake Fox, born 13 June, 1811; married, 1st, 1 July, 1841, Julianna E. Jennings, who died 19 April, 1842, *s. p.* He married, 2ndly, 30 October, 1851, Julianna Updegraff, who died 18 January, 1866. He died 5 November, 1859, having had issue by his 2nd wife—
        i. Charles Aubrey Fox, born 11 September, 1852.
        ii. Edward Updegraff Fox, born 9 April, 1856.
        i. Mary Anna Fox, born 25 September, 1854.
        ii. Elizabeth Wilson Fox, born 21 March, 1858.
        iii. Frances Drake Fox, born 14 May, 1860, and died 5 June, 1866.
    1. Elizabeth Miller Fox, married to M. W. Chapline (see p. 20).
    2. Anna Applebee Fox, married to Robert J. Curtis (see p. 21).
    3. Rebecca Steevens Fox, married to E. Pickering (see p. 21).
    4. Sarah Scantlebury Fox, married to B. E. Dungan (see p. 21).

(8.) Peter Applebee Fox, died 1771, unmarried.

(1.) Rebecca Fox married, 1783, to Joseph, son of Benjamin Cookworthy and Sarah Collier (see page 18), died *s.p.*

(2.) Jane Fox, married, 14 April, 1781, to William, son of Thomas Clark and Mary Franklin, who died 4 December, 1832; she died 15 December, 1835, and had issue—
    1. William Clark, born 1791; died 1806.

2. Thomas Baskerville Clark, married at Portsea, 20 April, 1824, Elizabeth, daughter of John and Jane Mason, and had issue John Franklin Clark, born at Tours, 25 March, 1826, and died 28 July, 1849, unmarried, and Jane Applebee Clark, who married her cousin, Alfred Hinton (see below).

3. John Franklin Clark, died young.

1. Mary Clark, died *s. p.*

2. Jane Applebee Clark, died 1869, aged 79.

3. Deborah Clark, married, 5 August, 1812, to John Lawrence Hinton, son of John Hinton, and his wife Amy. daughter of Joshua Hutchins and his wife Amy, daughter of Thomas Collier, brother to Joseph Collier, of Plymouth, who married Dorothy Fox (see page 16) and his wife Amy Smith, and had issue five sons and three daughters—
    i. William Clark Hinton, born 7 November, 1813, and died 17 April, 1837.
    ii. John Franklin Hinton, born 21 February, 1815, and died 31 October, 1846.
    iii. Alfred Hinton, married at St. Leonard's Church, Shoreditch, 31 July, 1845, his cousin, Jane Applebee Clark (before mentioned), and had one son and two daughters, viz., Frederick William Hinton, Mary Clark Hinton, and Jane Franklin Hinton.
    iv. Charles Fox Hinton, married at Peckham. 2nd November, 1848, Sarah, daughter of John Hamilton and his wife, Jane Newby, of Peckham, and has daughter, Sarah Elizabeth Hinton, born 25 October, 1851.
    . Frederick Hinton, b. 21 March, 1820, and d. 3 May, 1841.
    i. Caroline Hinton, married in London, 29 November, 1840, to Thomas, eldest son of Charles and Elizabeth Perrott, of Highgate, and has one son and four daughters, viz., Charles Thomas Perrott, Emmeline Fox Perrott, Maria Elizabeth Perrott, Caroline Jane Perrott, and Eleanor Augusta Perrott.
    ii. Elizabeth Jane Hinton.
    iii. Emmeline Hinton, born 26 June, 1823, *ob. enf.*

4. Sarah Fox Clark.   5. Anna Clark.

(3.) Lydia Fox, died *s. p.* 1762.

(4.) Margaret Fox, died 1828, aged 83.

JAMES FOX, of Plymouth, 4th son of John Fox (see p. 7), married Mary Bush, and had issue four sons and eight daughters—

(1.) James Fox, died *s. p.*   (2.) Charles Fox, died *s. p.*

(3.) James Fox, married, 1812, to Maria Grigg, who died 11 February, 1869. He died 5 February, 1860, having had issue two sons and two daughters—
    1. Francis Fox, of Plymouth, married in 1850, Jane Fortescue, and has had Madeline Herbert Fox, born 28 Dec., 1850; Herbert Francis Fox, born 4 June, 1853, and died Nov. following; Edward Francis Fox, born 21 Feb., 1856; Walter James Fox, born 28 Feb., 1857, and died 16 July, 1863.
    2. Jas. Fox, born 30 Jan., 1817, married 28 Mar., 1854, Ann Birdwood, and has a son, Sidney Birdwood Fox, born 4 Oct. 1855.
    1. Louisa Mary Fox, born 7 November, 1812, married 5 March, 1835, to George Shirley Kiernan, and has a daughter Augusta Maria Kiernan, born 5 March, 1836, and married, October, 1854, to Benjamin Adney.
    2. Caroline Fox, born 24 April, 1815.

(4.) Charles Fox, died *s. p.*

(1.) Priscilla Fox, died *s. p.*

(2.) Lydia Fox, married, 1787, to John Prideaux, eldest son of George Prideaux, of Kingsbridge, solicitor, by his third wife, and had issue—
    1. John Prideaux, died *s. p.*; 2. Lydia Prideaux, born 1789, living 1872; 3. Jane Prideaux, died *s. p.*; 4. Mary Prideaux, died *s. p.*; 5. George James Prideaux, died *s. p.*; 6. Susan Prideaux, died *s. p.*; 7. Sarah Prideaux, died *s. p.*

(3.) Elizabeth Fox, died *s. p.*

(4.) Priscilla Fox, married, 1791, to John Petty Dearman, of Birmingham, and had issue five sons and four daughters—
    1. John James Dearman, died *s. p.* 1868; 2. Richard Dearman, died *s. p.*; 3. Edward Dearman, married J. L. M.

Elliot, no issue; 4. Charles Dearman, living unmarried; 5. Henry Dearman, died *s. p.* 1849; 1. Anna Dearman, died young; 2. Mary Dearman, married to George B. Lloyd, Esq., of Birmingham, and left two sons, viz., Sampson Samuel Lloyd, Esq., and George Braithwaite Lloyd, Esq., of Birmingham (*see* page 26); 3. Caroline Dearman, died *s. p.* 1852; and 4. Eliza Jane Dearman, married to William Janson, of Tottenham, and has had 4 sons and 7 daughters

  i. John William Janson, married Louisa Burnand, and has four sons and six daughters, viz.:—*i.* Henry Martyn Janson; *ii.* Francis William Janson; *iii.* John Henry Janson; *iv.* Percy Janson; *i.* Ellen Louisa Janson; *ii.* Sophia Janson; *iii.* Mary Beatrice Janson; *iv.* Evelyn Janson; *v.* Ethel Janson; *vi.* Frances Janson.

  ii. Frederick William Janson, died *s. p.* 1863.

  iii. Dearman Janson; *iv.* Charles Albert Janson.

  i. Mary Janson, married, at Winchmore Hill, 30th August, 1850, to George, eldest son of George Stacey, and his wife, Deborah Lloyd. He died 22nd May, 1858, and she died 22nd December, 1866, having had—*i.* George Stacey, born 2nd December, 1858; *i.* Eliza Jane; *ii.* Anna Maria; and *iii.* Eleanor Stacey.

  ii. Caroline Janson, died 1864. iii. Louisa Janson.

  iv. Jane Eliza Janson, married, at Winchmore Hill, 29th July, 1858, to Samuel, eldest son of Samuel Lloyd, of Wednesbury, and has two sons and nine daughters—*i.* Samuel Janson Lloyd, born 17th March, 1870; *ii.* Albert William Lloyd; *i.* Amy; *ii.* Edith Mary; *iii.* Adelaide Jane; *iv.* Charlotte; *v.* Caroline Janson; *vi.* Margaret Jessie; *vii.* Florence Annie; *viii.* Julia; and *ix.* Maria Lloyd.

  v. Ellen Sophia Janson.

  vi. Margaret Janson, married to John Nathaniel Smith, and has two sons—*i.* Frederick Gordon Soloman Smith; and *ii.* Leonard William Smith.

(5.) Susannah Rogers Fox, died *s. p.*

(6.) Catherine Fox, died *s. p.*

(7.) Mary Fox, died unmarried, 1852.

(8.) Margaret Fox, died unmarried.

COLLIER OF PLYMOUTH.

JOSEPH COLLIER, of Plymouth, second son of Thomas Collier, of Gryndle, in Colyton Rawleigh, county Devon, married Dorothy, third daughter of Francis Fox, of St. Germans (see page 7), who died in 1759. He died in 1764, having had six sons and nine daughters—

(1.) Joseph Collier, married to Mary Elworthy, and died 1773 *s. p.*

(2.) Benjamin Collier, of the Victualling Office, Deptford, married Katharine, daughter of Robert Reynolds, of Farringdon, county Berks, and left an only daughter, Mary Collier, who married Abraham De Horne (see that family, next page).

(3.) John Collier (see below).

(4.) Thomas Collier, died *s. p.*, 1762.

(5.) Jonathan Collier, died *s. p.*

(6.) Frederick Collier, died *s. p.*, 1762.

(1.) Harriet Collier, married to William Freeman, died *s. p.*

(2.) Elizabeth Collier, died *s. p.*, 1722.

(3.) Sarah Collier, married to Benjamin Cookworthy (see page 18).

(4.) Mary Collier, died *s. p.* 1724.

(5.) Jenny Collier, died *s. p.* 1804, aged 78.

(6.) Amy Collier, married in 1763 to Joseph Pike, and died *s. p.*

(7.) Elizabeth Collier, died *s. p.*

(8.) Anne Collier, died *s. p.*

(9.) Rachel Collier, married to John Hingston (see page 18).

JOHN COLLIER, just mentioned, third son of Joseph Collier, married, first, Anna, daughter of   Debell, of Looe, county Cornwall, who died *s. p.* He married, secondly, in 1760, Martha Padley, who died in 1780, having had six sons and three daughters—

(1.) Robert Collier, died *s.p.*

(2.) Joseph Collier, died *s.p.*

(3.) John Collier, formerly M.P. for Plymouth (see below).

(4.) Sylvanus Collier, died *s. p.*

(5) William Collier, married in 1798, Mary, daughter of James and Mary Hingston, who died in 1851, having had one son and four daughters—

  1. William Collier, died *s. p.*

  1. Mary Hingston Collier, living unmarried.

  2. Martha Collier, living unmarried.

  3. Charlotte Collier, married to Edward, son of Silvanus and Ann James, of Redruth, Cornwall, and had two sons and three daughters—

    i. William Collier James, born 29 December, 1839.

    ii. Edward Hamilton James, born 5 October, 1843.

    i. Charlotte Mary James, married to John Brown James, of Brucefield, Truro.

    ii. Martha Jane James.

    iii. Edith Anne James.

  4. Susan Collier, died unm.

(6.) Joseph Collier, died *s. p.*

(1.) Mary Collier, died *s. p.*

(2.) Susannah Collier, died *s.p.*

(3.) Jane Collier, died *s.p.*

JOHN COLLIER, of Grimstone, county Devon, third son of John Collier, just mentioned, M.P. for Plymouth, 1832-1841, J.P. and D.L., married in 1816, Emma, daughter of Robert Porrett, Esq., of North Hill House, Plymouth, and died 27 February, 1849, having had six sons and three daughters—

(1.) Sir Robert Porrett Collier, Knight, of whom presently.

(2.) William Padley Collier, died young.

(3.) William Frederick Collier, married Cycill Christiana, daughter of Charles Biggs Calmady, Esq., J.P. and D.L., of Langdon Court, county Devon, and has issue four sons and one daughter—

  1. Charles Calmady Collier; 2. Frederick Mortimer Collier; 3. George Buller Collier; 4. Harry William Collier; 1. Bertha Cycill Collier.

(4.) Mortimer John Collier, married 1st, Mary Elizabeth, daughter of Sir William Snow Harris, Knight, F.R.S., who died   He married 2ndly, on 30th March, 1871, Sophy Luddington, youngest daughter of John Whipple, Esq., and has— Sibyl Ernestine Collier.

(5.) John Francis Collier, Barrister-at-Law, married Frances-Anne-Jane, daughter of Robert-Francis Jenner, Esq., of Wenvoe Castle, county Glamorgan, J.P. and D.L., and has one son and two daughters—

  1. Hugh Collier.

  1. Maud Collier; 2. Rose Collier.

(6.) Arthur Bevan Collier, married Eliza Blaker, and has two daughters—

  1. Amy Collier; 2. Lilian Collier, unmarried.

(1.) Elizabeth Anna Collier, married to Colonel James Kennard Pipon, Deputy Assistant Adjutant-General, who died 7 June, 1868, and has three sons and two daughters—

  1. James Collier Clement Pipon, married; 2. Harry Pipon; 3. John Pakenham Pipon; 1. Emma Jane Pipon; 2. Edith Philippa Pipon, married to Captain Pownall.

(2.) Jane Padley Collier, died young.

(3.) Emma Collier, died young.

THE RIGHT HON. SIR ROBERT PORRETT COLLIER, Knight, Q.C., of Grimstone and London (created 1863), born 1817, married 19th April, 1844, Isabella, daughter of William Rose Rose, Esq., of Woolston Heath, county of Warwick. Educated at Trinity College, Cambridge (B.A. 1841); called to the Bar at the Inner Temple, 1843, and went the Western Circuit; is a J.P. and D.L. for Devon; late Recorder for Penzance; and Judge Advocate of the Admiralty Court; was Solicitor-General 1863-6, Attorney-General 1868-71, was appointed a Judge of the Privy Council, November, 1871, and was M.P. for Plymouth since 1852-71. He has two sons and one daughter—

(1.) Robert Collier, born 1845.   (2.) John Collier, born 1850.

(1.) Margaret Collier, born 1847.

DE HORNE OF STANWAY.

ABRAHAM DE HORNE, of Surrey Square, eldest son of George de Horne, Esq., of Stanway Hall, county Essex, and his wife, Sarah Blewett, was born 2 January, 1762, and married 19 April, 1786, Mary, only daughter of Benjamin Collier (*see preceding page*), who died 25 November, 1823. He died 17 July, 1830, having had four sons and three daughters—

(1.) George de Horne, of Stanway Hall, born 27 January, 1788.
(2.) Benjamin Collier de Horne, of Farringdon, born 1 December, 1790, married, 23 February, 1814, Mary, daughter of Thomas Huntley, Esq., of Burford, Oxon, and died 25 July, 1858, leaving an only daughter—

   1. Katharine Collier de Horne, married, first, 8 July, 1841, to George Bevington, Esq., of Dulwich Lodge, Surrey, who died 7 October, 1866 ; secondly, 25 August, 1870, to Alfred Christy, Esq.

(3.) John de Horne, of Camberwell, born 1792, married, 27 October, 1819, Sarah, daughter and co-heiress of Thomas Manning, Esq., of Poole, Dorset, and died *s. p.* 23 June, 1821. She married secondly, Captain Henry Festing, R.A., elder brother of Rear-Admiral Robert Festing, C.B.
(4.) Abraham de Horne, of whom presently.
(1.) Katharine de Horne, married, 15 October, 1807, to Alfred Smith, Esq., of Earls Colne, Essex, and dying 5 August, 1847, left issue, Maria de Horne Smith, married, 31 October, 1833, to William Woodward, Esq., and has issue.
(2.) Sarah de Horne, married, 20 October, 1812, to John Christy, Esq., of Apuldrefield, Kent, third son of Miller Christy, Esq., who was born 19 June, 1781. She died 31 March, 1869, having had seven sons and three daughters—

   1. John de Horne Christy, born 25 August, 1814, married, 21 July, 1842, Ann, daughter of Robert Kidder, of Westerham, and died 1 August, 1850, having had two sons and two daughters. His widow died 24 October, 1852.
   2. Alfred Christy, of Lewisham, county Kent, born 14 January, 1818, married Katharine Collier de Horne, mentioned above.
   3. George Christy, born 11 April, 1819.
   4. Edward Christy, of Farringdon, Berks., born 6 June, 1820, married, 31 August, 1847, Julia Shears, daughter of Charles Spurrell, Esq., of Hill House, Dartford, and died *s. p.* 4 May, 1850.
   5. Frederick Collier Christy, of Melbourne, born 9 September, 1822, married, 18 April, 1861, Caroline, daughter of Arthur B. Wells, Esq., of Melbourne, and has issue a daughter.
   6. Arthur de Horne Christy, of Edenbridge, Kent, born 6 August, 1828, married, 14 September, 1865, Harriet Charlotte, daughter of Henry Chetwynd, Esq., of Brocton Lodge, county Staffordshire, and fourth son of Sir George Chetwynd, Bart., and has issue.
   7. Albert Christy, born 21 March, 1830; Captain 10th Madras N. I.
   1. Sarah Christy, died 21 September, 1825.
   2. Emma Catherine Collier Christy, married, 2 February, 1836, to George Steinman Steinman, Esq., F.S.A., of Sundridge, county Kent, and has—

      i. Matravers Harcourt Collier Bernhard Steinman, Captain R.H.A., born 13 April, 1839, married, 24 April, 1867, Jane Harriet, daughter of Richard Puckle, Esq., of Broadwater, county Sussex.
      i. Ellen Gertrude de Horne Christy Steinman, married, 20 August, 1862, William Kemmis, Esq., Captain R.A., and has issue.
      ii. Emma Isabella de Horne Christy Steinman.
   3. Ellen Maria Christy, died 2 May, 1833.
(3.) Mary de Horne, died 4 November, 1860.

ABRAHAM DE HORNE, of Lexden, Essex, fourth and youngest son of Abraham de Horne, and his wife, Mary Collier (above mentioned), born 8 May, 1796, married, first, 6 Nov., 1813, Mary, daughter of Josiah Wild, Esq., of Camberwell, who died 16 November, 1827, having had four sons and three daughters—

(1.) John Wild de Horne, born 26 February, 1815, married, 22 March, 1838, Maria, daughter of Thomas Gotsall, and died 5 September, 1870, leaving with four daughters, two sons—

   1. John de Horne, born 29 August, 1842.
   2. Morris de Horne, born 31 March, 1844.

(2.) George de Horne, born 9 September, 1820, died 13 September, 1847.
(3.) Abraham de Horne, born 11 April, 1822, died 2 January, 1836.
(4.) Thomas de Horne, born 3 February, 1824, married, 13 October, 1859, Emma, daughter of Walter Johnson, Esq., of Colchester.
(1.) Emily de Horne, married 18 June, 1834, to Henry Waddilove Best, Esq., of Thetford, Norfolk, who died 30 July, 1865. She died 27 October, 1857, having issue.
(2.) Louisa de Horne, married 1 August, 1844, to Alexander Bevington, Esq., of Roupell House, Streatham, and has issue.
(3.) Mary de Horne, married 24 February, 1848, to Dennis de Berdt Hovell, Esq., of Lower Clapton, and has issue.
Abraham de Horne married secondly, 21 June, 1835, Eliza, daughter of William Henry Butler, Esq., and died 18 April, 1867, having had three sons and six daughters—

(5.) Abraham de Horne, born 1846.
(6.) William Henry de Horne, born 1850.
(7.) Stewart de Horne, born 1852.
(4.) Eliza Emmeline de Horne.
(5.) Ada de Horne, married 14 June, 1859, to John Crompton Todd, Esq., and has issue.
(6.) Jessie, died 18 April, 1841.
(7.) Rosalind de Horne, married 11 November, 1868, to Edmund Phillips, Esq.
(8.) Jane, died 24 January, 1849.
(9.) Katharine de Horne.

PRIDEAUX OF KINGSBRIDGE.

GEORGE PRIDEAUX, born 1744, son of George Prideaux, married Anna, daughter of Philip Cookworthy, and his wife Rachel Botters, *née* Debell (see next page), and had five sons and four daughters—

(1.) George Prideaux, died unmarried.
(2.) Philip Cookworthy Prideaux, married 28 March, 1799, Esther, daughter of Jonathan Bawden and Anna Tuckett, (see page 20), and had Philip Cookworthy Prideaux, George Prideaux, and Anna Bawden Prideaux.
(3.) William Prideaux married Mary Cowles Anstice, who died 1868, and has had two sons and eight daughters—Francis William Prideaux, Beville Prideaux, Emma Beesley Prideaux, Ellen Prideaux, Louisa Prideaux, Caroline Prideaux, Elizabeth Prideaux, Isabella Prideaux, Fanny Prideaux, Annette Prideaux.
(4.) Walter Prideaux married Sarah Ball Hingston, daughter of Joseph Hingston and Sarah Ball (see next page), and had six sons and five daughters—

   1. Walter Prideaux, married Elizabeth, daughter of General Williams, and has issue, two sons and three daughters—
      i. Walter Sherborne Prideaux. ii. Arthur R. Prideaux.
      i. Ellen E. Prideaux, married to Lieut. Wace, R.A. ; died *s. p.* ii. Ada Hollond Prideaux. iii. Sarah T. Prideaux.
   2. Charles Prideaux, married, first, Elizabeth Abbott, and second, Elizabeth Wakefield, and has no issue.
   3. Henry Prideaux, married Agnes, daughter of Robert Morris, and has issue, three sons and six daughters—
      i. Henry Maxwell Prideaux. ii. Walter Baldwin Prideaux. iii. Robert Morris Prideaux.
      i. Agnes Prideaux. ii. Amy Henrietta Prideaux. iii. Edith Kara Prideaux. iv. Mabel Prideaux. v. Augusta Prideaux. vi. Fanny Claudia Prideaux.
   4. Alfred Prideaux, married Ann, daughter of Nicholas Vivian, and has—with Vivian, Edward, Charles, and Clara Allen Prideaux, all of whom died young—one son and three daughters—
      i. Rev. Walter Alfred Prideaux, married Elizabeth Lovey Lawrence.

i. Julia Anne Prideaux, married to Geo. Samuel Collins.
ii. Sarah Ball Prideaux.
iii. Kathleen Vivian Prideaux.
5. Frederick Prideaux, married Fanny, daughter of Richard Ball, and has no issue.
6. Joseph Hingston Prideaux, died unmarried, 1840.
1. Sarah Anna Prideaux, married her cousin, S. P. Tregelles, (see below), and has no issue.
2. Susan Rachel Prideaux, married Charles Pridham, and has issue, six sons and four daughters—
  i. Charles Pridham. ii. Walter Prideaux Pridham, married Emma Mairs. iii. Arthur Edward Pridham. iv. Frederick James Pridham. v. Theodore Pridham. vi. Ernest Pridham.
  i. Caroline Pridham. ii. Augusta Pridham. iii. Sarah Hingston Pridham. iv. Maria Dawkins Pridham.
3. Augusta Prideaux, unmarried.
4. Lucy Prideaux, unmarried.
5. Emily Ball Prideaux, married Francis C., son of Richard Ball, and has issue three sons and one daughter—
  i. Richard Francis Ball. ii. Frederick Henry Ball. iii. Arthur Herbert Ball.
  i. Emily Caroline Ball.
(5.) Charles Prideaux, died *s. p.*
(1.) Anna Prideaux, died *s. p.*
(2.) Sarah Prideaux, married to Robert Phillips Fox (see page 8).
(3.) Dorothy Prideaux, married to Samuel, son of Samuel Tregelles and Rebecca Smith (see next page), and has—
  1. Samuel Prideaux Tregelles, LL.D., of Plymouth, married his cousin, Sarah Anna Prideaux, above mentioned.
  1. Anna Rebecca Tregelles. 2. Dorothea Tregelles, died *s. p.*
(4.) Rachel Cookworthy Prideaux, married to Robert Were Fox, (see page 10).

COOKWORTHY.

WILLIAM COOKWORTHY, of Plymouth (see page 62), married, 1704, Edith, daughter of John and Mary Debell (see that family, next page), and had four sons, viz :—
(1.) William Cookworthy, had issue, Lydia, Susanna, Mary, and Sarah Cookworthy, who married Francis, third son of George Fox, of Par, by his second wife Anna, daughter of Philip Debell, and had issue (see page 11).
(2.) Philip Cookworthy, married Rachel, widow of William Botters and daughter of Philip Debell and his wife Sarah Fox (see next page), who died in 1791. He died in 1775, having had three sons and two daughters—
  1. Philip Cookworthy, died *s.p.*; 2. Joseph Cookworthy, died *s.p.*; 3. William Cookworthy, died *s.p.*
  1. Anna Cookworthy, married George Prideaux, of Kingsbridge, and had nine children (see that family, page 17).
  2. Rachel Cookworthy, died *s.p.*
(3.) Jacob Cookworthy, married Sarah Morris.
(4.) Benjamin Cookworthy, next mentioned.

BENJAMIN COOKWORTHY, son of the above William Cookworthy, married Sarah, daughter of Joseph Collier and Dorothy Fox (see page 16), who died in 1777. He died October, 1785, having had, with five children who died in infancy—(1.) William Cookworthy, died, 1786, aged 36; (3.) Joseph Cookworthy (of whom presently); (5.) Sarah Cookworthy, died, 1814, aged 59; (6.) Benjamin Cookworthy, died, 1823, aged 66, unmarried, and (9.) Frederick Cookworthy, who married Sarah Ring, of Bristol, and had a son, Frederick Cookworthy, who married in 1820 his cousin, Mary Collier Cookworthy, mentioned on next col., who died in 1871. He died in 1849, aged 47, having had four children—
  1. William Cookworthy. 2. Joseph Cookworthy, married in France, where he now resides, and has eight children.
  1. Augusta Fox Cookworthy. 2. Emily Richardson Cookworthy.

JOSEPH COOKWORTHY, married first, Rebecca, daughter of John Fox, of Plymouth, and his wife Rebecca Steevens (see page 15), who died 1788, age 37, having had three daughters—
(1.) Hannah Collier Cookworthy, died 1792, aged 8.
(2.) Lydia Cookworthy, died 1800, aged 14.
(3.) Mary Collier Cookworthy, married to her cousin, Frederick Cookworthy, before mentioned.
And secondly, in 1790, Mary Robins, who died in 1837, aged 84. He died in 1833, having had three sons—
(1.) Joseph Collier Cookworthy, of whom presently.
(2.) William Cookworthy, died 1800, age 7.
(3.) John Cookworthy married Charlotte, daughter of Captain Peter Spicer, R.N., who married, secondly, to J. G. Bussell, and died 1835, aged 40, having had four children—1. William Spicer Cookworthy, formerly Capt. Royal Scots, and 60th Rifles, and and now Deputy Governor of Portland Prison, married Emily Ellen, daughter of the late Thos. Graham, Esq. 2. Edith Cookworthy, married to Rev. A. P. Sanderson. 3. Frances Cookworthy, living unmarried at Swan River; and 4. Josephine Cookworthy, died *s. p.*

JOSEPH COLLIER COOKWORTHY, M.D., of Plymouth eldest son of the above Joseph Cookworthy, married Jane, second daughter of John Urquhart, of Nairnshire, N.B., captain of H.M.'s 79th Foot, who died 1840. He married, secondly, the widow of the Rev. John Lloyd Lugger, and died in 1869, aged 77, having had by his first marriage five sons and two daughters—
(1.) A son who died an infant.
(2.) Rev. Urquhart Cookworthy, Rector of Sandford Orcas, Somerset, married Elizabeth S. Bayley, daughter of James Bayley, Esq., J.P., Willaston Hall, Cheshire and Rumleigh, Devon.
(3.) John Cookworthy, who died 1837, aged 12.
(4.) Colin Cookworthy.
(5.) Joseph Cookworthy.
(1.) Mary Frances Cookworthy, married to Thomas Webster, Q.C., and has 1. Francis Joseph Webster, and 2. Helen Avice Webster.
(2.) Helen Cookworthy, who died 1842, aged 15.

HINGSTON OF HOLBETON.

JOHN HINGSTON, of Kingsbridge, born 1737, son of James and Elizabeth Hingston, of Holbeton, married, first, in 1760, Rachel, daughter of George Fox, of Par, by his second wife, Anna Debell, who died in 1761 (see page 11); married, second, in 1763, Rachel, daughter of Joseph Collier, by his wife Dorothy Fox (see page 16), and had with John, who died *s. p.* 1769, and Dorothy, who married Robert Were Fox (see page 10), a son—

JOSEPH HINGSTON, of Dodbrooke, county Devon, born in 1764, married first, 22 November, 1785, Sarah, daughter of Joseph Ball, of Bridgewater, who died in 1790, having had issue, with Sarah Ball Hingston, who married Walter Prideaux (see page 17), a son—
  Joseph Hingston, of Holbeton and Dodbrooke House, born 5 May, 1788, married, 8 September, 1825, Elizabeth Talwin, eldest daughter of James Kenway, of Bridport, who died 17 March, 1869. He died 6 February, 1852, and had three daughters—
    i. Eliza Anne Hingston, died *s. p.*
    ii. Caroline Elizabeth Hingston, died *s. p.*
    iii. Josephine Hingston, married 11 September, 1851, to Robert Dymond, Esq., of Exeter, and has issue—Caroline Anne Dymond, Arthur Hingston Dymond, and Josephine Elizabeth Dymond.
Joseph Hingston, married secondly, in 1796, Catharine Phillips Tregelles, daughter of Joseph Tregelles, of Falmouth, and his wife, Sarah Hingston (see next page), died 30 April, 1835, having had four sons and five daughters—

2. Frederick Collier Hingston, born 1803, and died 1810.
3. Charles Hingston, M.D., of whom presently.
4. Alfred Hingston, J.P., of Plymouth, married in 1831, Mary, daughter of James Barton Nottage, of Lancaster, and has had five sons and five daughters—
   i. Rev. Alfred Nottage Hingston, Vicar of Kingsbridge, married at Southsea, 24 January, 1872, Mary J., daughter of the late T. Harris, of Kingsbridge.
   ii. Joseph Tregelles Hingston, married, 1868, Emily Smith, and has one son—Alfred Alwyn Hingston.
   iii. Frederick Collier Hingston.
   iv. George Hingston.
   v. Augustus Hingston.
   i. Jane Catherine Hingston.
   ii. Mary Elizabeth Hingston, died *s. p.*
   iii. Esther Margaret Hingston.
   iv. Emma Rachel Hingston.
   v. Rosette Hingston, married to Reginald Dewing, and died *s. p.*
5. Edwin Hingston, died *s. p.*
2. Catharine Tregelles Hingston, married William Browne, of Torquay.
3. Rachel Collier Hingston, married George Fox, of Ford Park, Plymouth (see page 10).
4. Susannah Anna Hingston, died 1843.
5. Sophia Price Hingston, married, 1836, to Alfred, son of Benjamin Gilbert Gilkes, who died 1871 ; she died 1852, *s. p.*
6. Louisa Ellen Hingston, married, 1835, to Gilbert, son of Benjamin Gilbert Gilkes, who died 1863, *s. p.*

CHARLES HINGSTON, M.D., of Plymouth, second son of Joseph Hingston, by his second marriage, born 1805, married first, 1830, Mary, daughter of George Braithwaite, of Kendal, and by her had two daughters, who died *s. p.* He married secondly in 1837, Louisa Jane, daughter of Sir William George Parker, Bart., and by her has two sons and five daughters—
(1.) Charles Albert Hingston, M.D.
(2.) Ernest Alison Hingston, married in 1869, Mary Ellen, daughter of Theodore Davis, Esq., and has Charles Theodore Alison Hingston, and twin daughters, Margaret Alison Hingston and and Edith Alison Hingston.
(1.) Louisa Hingston, died 1858.
(2.) Charlotte Parker Hingston, married to W. F. Fox (see page 9).
(3.) Fanny Catherine Hingston, married in 1967, to Arthur J. Hill, son of Rev. R. Hill, of Bath, and has three daughters.
(4.) Clara Gertrude Hingston.
(5.) Sophia Elizabeth Hingston.

DEBELL OF LOOE.

ROBERT DEBELL, of St. Martin's, Looe, married, *circa* 1652, and appears to have died *circa* 1697, having had three sons and one daughter—
(1.) Robert Debell, born 1654, married, first, in 1681, Mary Peake, and secondly, in 1700 Grace Williams.
(2.) Philip Debell, of whom presently.
(3.) John Debell, married Mary ——, and had, with Ann, another daughter, Edith, who was married, 1704, to William Cookworthy, and had issue (see that family, page 18).
(1.) Edith Debell, married, 1679, to William Hancock, and had, with other issue, a son, William Hancock, who married Abigail Tuckett, and had issue (see that family, next page).

PHILIP DEBELL, above mentioned, born, 1657, married, first, —— Wilmoth, and by her had a son, Philip, and a daughter, Mary, who both died *s. p.* ; he married, secondly, Anna Soady, and had by her six sons and four daughters, viz.—
(1.) Joseph Debell, married, first, Margaret Diamond, and, second,

Susannah Cookworthy, and whose children died *s. p.*
(2.) Philip Debell, of Looe, born 1689, married, in 1712, Sarah, second daughter of Francis Fox, of St. Germans (see page 7), (she was born in 1690, and died in 1778), and had one son and two daughters—
   1. Philip Fox Debell, died *s. p.* 1718.
   1. Anna Debell, married to James Tuckett, of Newton, and afterwards of Looe, and had issue (see that family, next page).
   2. Rachel Debell, married, first, to William Botters, who died *s. p.* She married, second, to Philip Cookworthy, and had issue (see that family, on preceding page).
(3.) John Debell, married Mary Stephens, and had, with others, a daughter, Mary, married James Tuckett, of Newton (see next page).
(4.) Benjamin Debell, died young.
(5.) Benjamin Debell, married Amy Brooking, and left issue.
(6.) Robert Debell, died young.
(1.) Wilmoth Debell, married John Read, of St. Keyn, and had issue, all of whom died *s. p.*
(2.) Mary Debell, married Joseph Tregelles, of Falmouth, and had, with others—
   1. Joseph Tregelles, married Sarah Hingston, and had, with others, 1. Anna, who married Peter Price ; 2. Samuel, married Rebecca Smith, and had, with others, Samuel Tregelles, who married Dorothy Prideaux (see page 18), and Anne Peters Tregelles, who married Joseph Fox (see page 13); 3. Elizabeth Tregelles, who married Robert Were Fox (see page 11) ; 4. Mary Tregelles, who married Thomas Were Fox (see page 11); 5. Catherine Phillips Tregelles, who married Joseph Hingston (see page 18).
   2. Anna Tregelles, married Charles Peters, and had Elizabeth, who married Joseph Fox, of Falmouth (see pages 12 and 13).
(3.) Anna Debell, married to George Fox, of Par (see page 11).
(4.) Sarah Debell, married to Richard Wadge, of Wadebridge.

SKETCH OF THE TUCKETT'S OF DEVONSHIRE.

THERE is a tradition that this family is descended from Ormus le Citherista (*i.e.* Harper), alias Touchet, mentioned in Ormerod's "History of Cheshire," as coming over with William the Conqueror, and as the son of one of his barons. This tradition of the origin of the family is somewhat strengthened by Shakespeare—Henry V., Act iv., Scene 2, line 35 :—
  "Then let the trumpets sound
   The Tucket Sonuance and the note to mount ;"
The various branches of the family have always borne for arms a chevron between three crosses ; the tinctures have varied as the exact spelling of the name has. Those borne by their branch were confirmed at Herald's College, in the last century, as follows :—Or, a chevron between three crosses, azure; crest, a Holy Lamb, couchant, proper, having a flag charged with a cross, gules; motto—En Dieu est ma Fiance.

ELIAS TUCKETT, of Christow, near Chudleigh, was born in 1597; there is a certificate of his burial at that place on the 7th of November, 1697, at the age of ninety. He became a follower of George Fox, and is mentioned in Besse's "Sufferings of Friends" (vol. i., page 161) as eighty-one years old, blind and almost deaf, and imprisoned at Exeter for non-payment of tithes. His son, JAMES TUCKETT, is mentioned in "Leadbeater's Notices" (page 209) as ancient, blind, and a prisoner at Exeter, for tithes in 1732. He owned and resided at the Manor of Abbots Kerswell, an estate which a few generations later passed out of the family, with the exception of the private burial-ground, where the family and their friends were interred for several generations, and which was reserved and still belongs to his heirs. He had two sons and one daughter—
(1.) James Tuckett, married —— Sparkes, died *s. p.*
(2.) Elias Tuckett, of whom hereafter.

(3.) Abigail Tuckett, married to Jonah Binns, and had two sons—
 1. Thomas Binns, married Rachel Sparkes, and had three sons; Thomas Binns, William Binns, and Joseph Binns; and three daughters, Rachel Binns, Abigail Binns, and Elizabeth Binns.
 2. Jonathan Binns, married Anna Debell, in 1768, and had one son, Jonathan Binns, and two daughters, Anna Binns, and Frances Binns, who married Nicholas Were.

ELIAS TUCKETT, second son of Elias Tuckett, before mentioned, purchased and entailed a small estate called Underhaye, in the parish of Netherton, which has never since been alienated, but after the death of his father it is supposed he resided at Abbots Kerswell, which is not very distant. He had four sons and one daughter—
(1.) Elias Tuckett married Sarah Merchant, of Bath, about 1750, and had one daughter, Elizabeth Tuckett, who married Lieutenant-General Douglas Wemyss, and died *s. p.*
(2.) James Tuckett, of whom hereafter.
(3.) Henry Tuckett, died *s. p.*
(4.) William Tuckett, died *s. p.*
(1.) Abigail Tuckett, married to William, son of William Hancock and Edith Debell (see preceding page), and had one son and two daughters—
 1. William Hancock, went to America.
 1. Mary Tuckett Hancock, died *s. p.*
 2. Elizabeth Hancock, married J. Folle.

JAMES TUCKETT, second son of Elias, before mentioned, married, in 1742, Anna, daughter of Philip Debell, of Looe, in Cornwall (see preceding page), and thereupon removed to Looe. She having died, he married, in 1751, her first cousin, Mary, daughter of John Debell (see Debell pedigree on preceding page). By the former marriage he had two sons and three daughters—
(1.) James Tuckett, died *s. p.*
(2.) Philip Debell Tuckett, of whom presently.
(1.) Sarah Tuckett, died *s. p.*
(2.) Rachel Tuckett, died *s. p.*
(3.) Anna Tuckett, married, first, to Jonathan Bawden; second, to Charles Bawden, and had issue by her first marriage a daughter— Esther, married Philip Cookworthy Prideaux (see page 7).
James Tuckett had, by his second marriage, three sons and two daughters—
(1.) Elias Tuckett, died *s. p.*
(2.) James Tuckett, died *s. p.*
(3.) John Tuckett, of Bristol, married, first, Jane C. Helton; second, Hannah Beswick; and, third, Rachel Soady. By his first marriage he had seven sons and one daughter—
 1. John Tuckett married Hannah Bracher.
 2. Elias Helton Tuckett married Martha Bulgin, and has many descendants.
 3. Philip Debell Tuckett married Eleanor Harris, who died March, 1872, and left several sons and daughters.
 4. James Tuckett, died *s. p.*
 5. Charles Tuckett, died *s. p.*
 6. William Tuckett married Mary Fothergill, and has one son and one daughter.
 7. Edward Tuckett married ——, and left sons and daughters.
 1. Caroline Tuckett, married to William Cross, and had one son and two daughters.
(1.) Mary Tuckett, married to William Kale.
(2.) Sarah Tuckett, died *s. p.*

PHILIP DEBELL TUCKETT, of Frenchay, second and eldest surviving son of James Tuckett, of Looe, married, first, Esther Champion, and had Esther Champion Tuckett, who died *s. p.*, and married, secondly, in 1800, Elizabeth, daughter of William Curtis, of Alton, and widow of John Wright, banker, London, and by her had—
(1.) Philip Debell Tuckett, born at Frenchay in 1801; married, in 1832, Anna, daughter of Samuel Edmunds, of High Wycombe. He died 15th August, 1872, having had two sons—

1. Philip Debell Tuckett, born at Frenchay, 1833, married, in 1867, Rachel Elizabeth, widow of S. Lindoe Fox, and eldest daughter of Alfred Fox (see page 12), of Falmouth, and has two sons—
 i. Philip Debell Tuckett, born at Cleveland Gardens, London, in 1868.
 ii. Percival Fox Tuckett, born at Cleveland Gardens in 1870.
2. Samuel Edmunds Tuckett, born 1837, died 1861, *s. p.*
(2.) Francis Tuckett, born 1802, married Mariana, daughter of Robt. Were Fox (see page 11), and has issue—
 1. Francis Fox Tuckett, of Frenchay and Bristol.
 1. Elizabeth Fox Tuckett, died *s. p.*
 2. Elizabeth Fox Tuckett, married in March, 1871, to William Fowler, of Forest House, Leytonstone, M.P. for Cambridge, son of the late John Fowler, of Elm Grove, Corsham, Wilts, and died 31 May, 1872.
 3. Mariana Fox Tuckett, married to her cousin, Joseph Hoyland Fox, of Wellington, and has issue (see page 9).
 4. Charlotte Fox Tuckett, married at Wellington, Somerset, 13 December, 1871, to Eliot Howard, Esq., of Tottenham.
(3.) Alfred Tuckett, born 1804, married Helen, daughter of Samuel Curtis, and has four sons and two daughters.
(4.) Henry Tuckett, born 1806, and died *s. p.*
(5.) Frederick Tuckett, born 1807.

CHAPLINE, OF WHEELING, U.S

ELIZABETH MILLER FOX, eldest daughter of Josiah Fox, of Ohio (see page 15). Married Moses W. Chapline, of Wheeling, West Virginia, and has had five sons and eight daughters—
(1.) Alexander Hamilton Chapline, of Wheeling, born 15 October, 1813, married 12 November, 1840, Dorcas J. Dorsey, and has had three sons and seven daughters—
 1. Alexander Hamilton Chapline, born 18 September, 1845.
 2. Moses W. Chapline, born 20 June, 1851, and died 7 July following.
 3. Ely Dorsey Chapline, born 19 December, 1847, and died 24 April following.
 1. Elizabeth Miller Chapline, born 5 December, 1841, and died 30 December, 1864.
 2. Jane Stanton Chapline, born 21 October, 1843, and died 20 June, 1860.
 3. Mary Ann Pomeroy Chapline, born 29 March, 1849, married 21 December, 1871, to Samuel Purcell Norton.
 4. Ellen Forsyth Chapline, born 28 November, 1852, and died 1 June, 1860.
 5. Amelia Campbell Chapline, born 14 September, 1855.
 6. Anna Cora Chapline, born 19 February, 1858.
 7. Jessie Stanton Chapline, born 2 August, 1860, and died 14 December following.
(2.) Moses W. Chapline, married Margaret S. Thomas, and has Annie Terrell and Maggie Chapline.
(3.) William Henry Chapline, married Eliza de France Bradley, and has Frances Roberta, and (twins) Charles William and Elizabeth Mary Chapline.
(4.) Charles James Fox Chapline, born 1829, and died 16 December, 1866.
(5.) Francis Drake Fox Chapline.
(1.) Mary Ann Chapline, born 5 June, 1815, married 3 September, 1835, Josiah Wright Pomeroy, who died 15 June, 1866, having had one son and four daughters—
 1. Arthur Roby Pomeroy, born 29 October, 1847.
 1. Cora Pomeroy, born 15 June, 1836, married 30 September, 1861, to Grafton Dulaney Rogers, now of New York, and has—
  i. Henry Woodward Rogers, born 9 March, 1866.
  i. Mary Grafton Rogers, born 29 June, 1863.

2. Claudine Pomeroy, born 14 April, 1839, and died 17 April, 1841.
3. Lena Pomeroy, born 21 May, 1842, and died 16 August, 1849.
4. Mary Chapline Pomeroy, born 9 May, 1856.
(2.) Elizabeth Good Chapline, married Percival M. Potts, now of San Francisco, and has two sons and two daughters—
    1. Charles Potts; 2. William Potts.
    1. Virginia Potts, born 24 October, 1863.
    2. Nina Potts, married Alphonso F. Tilden (2nd wife), now of Brooklyn, New York, and has two sons and one daughter—
      i. John Maxwell Tilden, born 29 July, 1865.
      ii. Alphonso Tilden, born 3 May, 1869.
      i. Nina Tilden, born 16 December, 1871.
(3.) Maria Louise Chapline, married 28 March, 1853, Jonathan C. Lawrence, now of Salt Lake City, and has had three daughters—
    1. Lucy Chapline Lawrence, born 15 January, 1855, and died 17 July, 1859.
    2. Rowena Caldwell Lawrence, born 6 September, 1858, and died 7 August, 1859.
    3. Lulu Mary Lawrence, born 19 June, 1861, and died 27 July following.
(4.) Jane Ralph Chapline, married 1st, in 1843, to Robert Stanton, who died 1853, and 2ndly, in 1857, to Frederick Stanton, of Natchez, Mississippi, and has issue by 1st marriage, Elizabeth Brandon Stanton, born 1851; and Hulda May Stanton, born 1853; by 2nd marriage, Lenox Surget Stanton, born 1854; Frederick Maud Stanton, born 1865; Jane Ralph Chapline Stanton, born 1860, and Anna Linn Chapline Stanton, born 1863, and died 1869.
(5.) Sophia Jane Chapline, married 4 September, 1853, Alphonso F. Tilden (who married 2ndly, Nina Potts, see *ante*), and died 27 November, 1862, leaving two sons—
    1. Charles W. Tilden, born 19 January, 1857.
    2. Henry Bates Tilden, born 25 June, 1859.
(6.) Josephine Isabella Chapline, married Thomas B. Roby, and has issue, Elizabeth Chapline Roby and Frederick Stanton Roby.
(7.) Anna Corinna Chapline.
(8.) Rowena Caldwell Chapline, born 15 October, 1840, married in 1867, to Charles P. Robbins, and died 27 July, 1869, having had, Mary Rowena Robbins, born 1868, and Charles P. Robbins, born July, 1869.

CURTIS, OF MOUNDSVILLE, U.S.

ANNA APPLEBEE FOX, second daughter of Josiah Fox, of Ohio (see page 15), married 24 September, 1822, Robert J. Curtis, of Moundsville, West Virginia, and has had issue—
(1.) Charles Fox Curtis, born 31 March, 1825, and died 1 July, 1834.
(2.) George Douglas Curtis, of Moundsville, born 29 December, 1826, married 9 October, 1860, Cynthia Anna Riggs, and has had three sons—
    1. William Riggs Curtis, born 2 June, 1863.
    2. Irene Oldham Curtis, born 12 April, 1866.
    3. Charles Curtis, born 8 October, 1870, and died 1 October, 1871.
(3.) Robert Bonham Curtis, born 3 December, 1830.
(4.) Josiah Fox Curtis, born 5 December, 1832, married 26 March, 1868, Landorria Lorentz, and has a daughter, Anna Lorentz Curtis, born 30 January, 1869.
(1.) Mary Curtis, born 15 July, 1823, married 23 May, 1844, Wylie H. Oldham, of Marietta, Ohio, and has had six sons and two daughters—
    1. Douglas Jerrold Oldham, born 9 November, 1845, and died 16 December following.
    2. Irene Oldham, born 27 October, 1846, died 30 January, 1866.
    3. Frank Fox Oldham, born 4 March, 1849.

    4. Charles Russell Oldham, born 15 November, 1852.
    5. George Curtis Oldham, born 13 April, 1856.
    6. Wylie Edward Oldham, born 7 October, 1860.
    1. Ellen Caldwell Oldham, born 19 December, 1850, and died 24 December, 1851.
    2. Mary Louise Oldham, born 11 June, 1862.
(2.) Elizabeth Chapline Curtis, born 22 October, 1828.

PICKERING, OF EAST RICH-LAND, U.S.

REBECCA STEVENS FOX, third daughter of Josiah Fox of Ohio (see page 15), married to Elijah Pickering, now of East Richland, Belmont, Ohio, and has had issue five sons and two daughters—
(1.) Henry Fox Pickering, of East Richland, born 19 December, 1827, married 10 May, 1862, Hannah Cook, and has issue—
    1. Joseph H. Pickering, born 22 August, 1866.
    1. Laura C. Pickering, born 10 June, 1863.
(2.) Josiah Fox Pickering, born 23 July, 1834, married 12 May, 1864, Rebecca J. Coppock, and has issue—
    1. Elijah C. Pickering, born 25 February, 1868.
    1. Anna Virginia Pickering, born 9 February, 1865.
(3.) John Charles Pickering, born 23 July, 1834.
(4.) Francis Drake Pickering, born 4 March, 1839, died 9 March 1844.
(5.) Hamilton Chapline Pickering, born 18 June, 1841, and died 22 February, 1844.
(1.) Anna Miller Pickering, born February, 1830, married 6 February, 1865, Dillon Pickering, and has had one son and two daughters—
    1. Charles James Fox Pickering, born 20 May, 1867, and died 24 September following.
    1. Mary Emma Lorena Pickering, born 10 October, 1865.
    2. Sarah Rebecca Pickering, born 28 May, 1870.
(2.) Sarah Fox Pickering, born 23 March, 1832, married William H. Seaman, and has had three sons and five daughters—
    1. Isaac Hamilton Seaman, born 30 July, 1854.
    2. William H. Seaman, born 12 February, 1863.
    3. Jno. Charles Seaman, born 6 June, 1869, and died 12 March, 1870.
    1. Anna Miller Seaman, born 29 March, 1856.
    2. Mary List Seaman, born 2 November, 1858.
    3. Rebecca Fox Seaman, born 18 November, 1860.
    4. Elizabeth Caroline Seaman, born 6 April, 1866, and died 28 May, 1867.
    5. Sarah Dungan Seaman, born 5 April, 1871.

DUNGAN, OF COLERAIN, U.S.

SARAH SCANTLEBURY FOX, fourth and youngest daughter of Josiah Fox, of Ohio (see page 15), married 30 May, 1833, to Benjamin Ellis Dungan, now of Colerain, Belmont, Ohio, and has had four sons and four daughters—
(1.) Josiah Fox Dungan, born 10 March, 1834, and died 8 May, 1861.
(2.) Charles James Dungan, born 8 October, 1836, married Susan G. Lemmon, and has two sons and one daughter—
    1. Ellis Wilson Dungan, born 30 November, 1867.
    2. Charles Francis Dungan, born 15 August, 1871.
    1. Sadie Blanche Dungan, born September, 1869.
(3.) William Henry Dungan, born 4 June, 1838.
(4.) Thomas Corwin Dungan, born 3 April, 1840.
(1.) Mary Anne Dungan, born 16 June, 1841.
(2.) Elizabeth Chapline Dungan, born 7 July, 1843, married Isaac G. Cope, and has two sons and one daughter—
    1. Caleb Herman Cope, born 5 April, 1868.
    2. Ellis Corwin Cope, born 26 November, 1869.
    1. Marianna Cope, born 1 March, 1871.

(3.) Julia Updegraff Dungan, born 9 January, 1845, married John A. Leash, and has had one son and two daughters—
1. Ellis D. Leash, born 12 May, 1869.
1. Lizzie B. Leash, born 4 July, 1866.
2. Sadie D. Leash, born 26 October, 1867, and died 16 December following.
(4.) Sarah Conrad Dungan, born 9 May, 1847.

ELLICOTT FAMILY.

MARY, eldest daughter of Francis Fox, of St. Germans, by his 2nd wife, Tabitha Croker (see page 7), born 1686, married, 1707, Andrew Ellicot of Collumpton, son of Andrew and Elizabeth Ellicot, and died 1759. He removed to America with his eldest son, having had by Mary Fox two sons and one daughter—
(1.) Andrew Ellicot (see next page). (2.) Joseph Ellicot, d. 1751.
(1.) Mary Ellicot, married, 1733, Nicholas Emmett, of Parr, co. Cornwall, who was born 1683. She died 1742, having had one daughter—
Elizabeth, married Clement Jackson, of Looe, Cornwall, and had one son—
Eliphas Jackson, married Hannah Westcombe, and had two sons and one daughter—
i. Eliphaz Jackson, died.
ii. Clement Jackson, of Looe, died.
i. Lucy, married William Enoch, of Hey, co. Brecon, and had two daughters—
1. Clementina. 2. Lucy, died.

ANDREW ELLICOT, eldest son of Andrew Ellicot, of Collumpton, married Ann Bye, and had, with Nathaniel, who died unmarried, four other sons—
(1.) Joseph Ellicot, married Judith Blater, and had four sons and five daughters—
1. Andrew Ellicot, married Sarah Brown, and had three sons and six daughters—
i. Andrew. ii. George; and iii. Joseph Ellicot.
i. Jane. ii. Mary. iii. Letitia, iv. Sarah. v. Nancy; and vi. Rachel Ellicot.
2. David Ellicot.
3. Joseph Ellicot [obtained great wealth as a surveyor of new lands].
4. Benjamin Ellicot.
1. Sarah Ellicot. 2. Ann Ellicot.
3. Letitia Ellicot, married John Evans, and had two sons and four daughters—
i. William Evans [inherited his uncle Joseph Ellicot's property], married Mary Randall, and is now dead. They had seven sons and one daughter—
i. John. *ii.* James. *iii.* Charles. *iv.* Benjamin. *v.* William. *vi.* Lewis; and *vii.* Andrew Evans.
i. Rachel Evans.
ii. Lewis Evans.
i. Rachel. ii. Ann. iii. Martha; and iv. Letitia Evans.
4. Rachel; and 5. Mary Ellicot.
(2.) * Andrew Ellicot, married, first, Elizabeth Brown, and had six sons and one daughter—
1. Jonathan Ellicot, married Sarah Harvey, and had six sons and six daughters—
i. Nathaniel Ellicot, died. ii. Samuel Ellicot.
iii. Nathaniel Ellicot. iv. William Ellicot.
v. Jonathan Ellicot. vi. Benjamin H. Ellicot.
i. Elizabeth Ellicot, married William E. George, and had—
i. Philip T. *ii.* Jonathan E. *iii.* Robert. *iv.* Harvey, and *v.* Francis George.
i. Eliza. *ii.* Anne. and *iii.* Mary Ann George.
ii. Sarah Ellicot, married William Tyson, clerk in the United States Treasury Department, Washington [now dead], and had six sons and four daughters—
i. Jonathan E. *ii.* William A. *iii.* Samuel. *iv.* Francis. *v.* Charles, and *vi.* Edward Tyson.

i. Sarah Ellicot Tyson, married Lloyd Norris [of Baltimore], and has issue.
ii. Mary. *iii.* Elizabeth. *iv.* Jane Norris.
iii. Frances Ellicot, died young. iv. Frances Ellicot.
v. Letitia Ellicot. vi. Mary Ann Ellicot.
2. Elias Ellicot, died young.
3. Elias Ellicot, married, 1786, Mary Thomas, and had eleven sons and four daughters—
i. Evan Ellicot, died.
ii. Evan T. Ellicot, married H. M. Bond; no issue.
iii. Benjamin Ellicot, of Baltimore.
iv. Thomas Ellicot (died), married Louisa McFadon, and had Priscilla.
v. Andrew Ellicot, of Baltimore, married Emily McFadon, and had—
i. William. *ii.* James. *iii.* Evan; and *iv.* John Ellicot.
vi. James Ellicot, died. vii. John Ellicot, married.
viii. Samuel Ellicot, married Mary Ann Todhunter, and had one daughter Eliza.
ix. Elias Ellicot, died *s. p.* x. Henry Ellicot, died *s. p.*
xi. Philip Ellicot [living 1852].
i. Elizabeth, married Lewin Wethered, of Baltimore, and had—
i. Peregrine Wethered, married Louisa Weeks.
ii. Charles Wethered, Member of Congress, married — Bathurst, of England.
iii. John Wethered [John and Charles are cloth manufacturers], married the daughter of Philip E. Thomas, and has no issue.
iv. Samuel Wethered.
v. Lewin Wethered.
i. Mary, married William G. Thomas, of Baltimore, and has a large family.
ii. Ann, married ———, United States Ambassador at Madrid, and has issue.
ii. Rachel, married John Hewes, and had—
i. Edward. *ii.* Elias. *iii.* Henry. *iv.* James. *v.* Benjamin; and *vi.* John Hewes.
i. Mary Hewes.
iii. Tacy, married Joseph King, of Baltimore, and had—
i. Francis King, of Baltimore, married, January 8, 1846, Elizabeth Taber, daughter of William C. Taber, of New Bedford, Massachusetts; she was born 1820.
ii. Thomas King [of San Francisco].
iii. Joseph King. *iv.* Elias King.
i. Mary King.
iv. Anne, died.

---

* Andrew Ellicot, married, secondly, Esther Brown, and had five sons and one daughter—
1. Joseph Ellicot, died.
2. James Ellicot, married H. Thomas, and had—
i. Charles Ellicot.
3. Andrew Ellicot, married Hannah Tunis, of Philadelphia, and had—
i. James; and i. Eliza Ellicot.
4. Thomas Ellicot, married Mary Miller [her father owned large estates in Chester County], and had—
i. William Ellicot, of Baltimore, married — Pulteney, and had issue—
i. Sarah Ann. *ii.* Hannah. *iii.* Lydia. *iv.* Mary. *v.* Rebecca. *vi.* Catherine. *vii.* Esther; and *viii.* Elizabeth Ellicot.
5. John Ellicot, married Mary, daughter of John Mitchell and Tacy Tyson, and had—
i. John Ellicot.
i. Rachel. ii. Ann; and iii. Mary Ellicot.
1. Tacy Ellicot, married Isaac Macpherson, of Baltimore (died), and had—
i. Esther. ii. Mary; and iii. Ann Macpherson.

4. George Ellicot, married Elizabeth Brooke, and had two sons and four daughters—
   i. James Ellicot, died.
   ii. George Ellicot, married ———— [Catholic lady].
   i. Elizabeth, married Thomas Lee, of Brandywine, and had issue.
   ii. Martha, married Nathan Tyson, of Baltimore [both living, 1852], and had—
     i. James Tyson [miller], married ————, of Virginia, and has issue.
     ii. Henry Tyson, married, ————, and had issue. [He lived at Gunpowder Falls, eighteen miles from Baltimore, the old house of the Tysons, in 1852.]
     iii. Robert Tyson. *iv.* Frederic Tyson.
     i. Elizabeth, married John Smith, druggist, of Baltimore, son of Matthew Smith, and had issue.
     ii. Ann Tyson.
   iii. Anna, the second wife of Thomas Tyson.
   iv. Mary, the first wife of Thomas Tyson, farmer, Montgomery County, Maryland, who had by her—
     Elizabeth, born about 1830.
5. Nathaniel Ellicot, married Elizabeth Ellicot [probably his first-cousin, and daughter of John Ellicot], and had—
   i. John Ellicot.
   ii. Nathaniel Ellicot, married, and had a daughter, who married ————, lawyer, of West Chester.
   iii. Jonathan Ellicot, in iron business, at Baltimore (1852).
   iv. Andrew Ellicot, married, in business with his brother.

   i. Hannah. ii. Cassandra ; and iii. Mary Ellicot.
6. Andrew Ellicot, died. 7. Elizabeth Ellicot.
(3.) Thomas Ellicot, married Ann Ely, and had—
   1. John. 2. Thomas; and 3. Joseph Ellicot.
   1. Ruth. 2. Sarah. 3. Ann. 4. Pamela; and 5. Letitia Ellicot.
(4.) John Ellicot, married, firstly, Leah Brown, and, secondly, Cassender Hopkinson. He had by one of these wives—
   1. John Ellicot. 2. Elizabeth; and 3. Hannah Ellicot.
   1. Martha Ellicot, married James Carey, of Baltimore, and had—
     i. John Carey, died.
     ii. Samuel Carey, married — Evans, of Buffalo, no issue.
     iii. John Ellicot Carey, married — Irvine, of Alexandria, and had—
       i. Thomas Carey [Presbyterian], married, 1852, Martha, daughter of George Leiper, of Leiperville, Delaware County, Pennsylvania.
       ii. James Carey, married ————, of New Bedford.
     iv. James Carey, died.
     v. George Carey, married ————, of Virginia, and had issue.
     i. Margaret, married Galloway Cheston, of Baltimore [no family].
     ii. Hannah, married William E. Coale, of Baltimore, and had five children, of which—
       1st. James Coale. 5th A daughter, born about 1834.
     iii. Martha, married Dr. Thomas, of Baltimore.

𝔓𝔢𝔡𝔦𝔤𝔯𝔢𝔢 𝔬𝔣 𝔱𝔥𝔢 ℭ𝔯𝔬𝔨𝔢𝔯𝔰.

Arms: Argent; a chevron engrailed gules between three ravens, two and one, p.p.r.

Crest: A drinking cup or, charged in the centre with a rose gules, and surmounted with three fleur-de-lis, p.p.r.

Motto: " J'ai ma foi tenu à ma puissance." It was also written formerly, " Je tiens ma foi à ma puissans;" and in right of the marriage of Tabitha Croker with Francis Fox, all the Fox family have the right to quarter the arms of Croker, and with them also those of Churchill and Bonvile.

The family of Croker, or Crocker, was one of the most ancient in Devonshire, being undoubtedly one of the old Saxon families. *Prince, in his " Worthies of Devon,"* remarks, " There is a " tradition in this county of three eminent families, that they were " settled here before the Conquest, according to that old saw, often " used among us in discourse,—

    ' Crocker, Crewys, and Coplestone,
      When the Conqueror came, were at home.' "

He also states that in his time, the then heir of his family, Courtenay Croker, of Lineham, had told him, " that when tra- " velling in Saxony, he met some gentlemen of his name, and that " they gave the same coat of arms as he doth, a plain argument " that originally they came out of that country." Their family seat for many generations was Lineham, in the parish of Yealhampton, co. Devon, brought to them by the marriage of a Sir John Croker, with Agnes, heiress of Giles Churchill, to whose ancestor it had been granted at the Conquest. By the marriage of Mary, daughter and heiress of Courtenay Croker, with James Bulteel, of Flete, it passed into that family, and it lately has been sold by their representative to Mr. Bastard, of Kitley. Originally, the Crokers lived at a place called Crocker's Hele, in the parish of Meeth, or Methe, four miles from Hatherleigh, Devon. They formed numerous marriages with some good Norman and Saxon

families, such as *Churchill, Pollard, Fortescue, Bonvile, Strode, Coplestone, Yeo, &c., &c.* " Their genealogy," says Mr. Burke, " is preserved with wonderful accuracy by Prince, Risdon, Pole, " and the other Devonshire historians, as well as by numerous " pedigrees and documents." This sketch is taken chiefly from Prince's " Worthies of Devon," particularly the note to the quarto edition, 1810, article Croker; Westcote's " Devonshire " Pedigrees;" Risdon's " Survey of Devon ;" Pole's " Devon ;" Burke's " History of the Commoners ;" various references to the Harleian MSS. in the British Museum, and some coats of arms on an old screen that formerly stood in the church of Yealhampton, Devon.

The first of the name of whom we have any account is William Crocker, of Crocker's Hele, in the parish of Meeth, Devonshire. He lived about 1307, and left a son, William Crocker, of Hele, temp. Edward III. His son, Sir John Croker, of Hele, married Agnes, daughter and heiress of Giles Churchill, of Lineham (*see Churchill*). They left Sir John Croker, of Lineham, who married the heiress of Corim,* and had a son, Sir John Croker, of Lineham and Hemerdon, who married the heiress of Dawnay † (Sir William

---

* The Manor of Hemerdon gave name to an ancient family who held it until the year 1296. In 1396, John Croker, of Lineham, became possessed of it by marriage with the " heiress of Corim." —*Lysons' " Devon," page* 413.

† Sir William Pole makes this Sir John Croker to have married Agnes Churchill. This, however, is a mistake, that marriage having really taken place with his grandfather. It is probably here that the marriage with " Dawnay " occurred, as the arms in Yealhampton Church proved this to have preceded that with the Pollards. In that church there was formerly a shield impaled, showing, therefore, husband and wife. Dexter, quarterly, 1. Croker; 2. Churchill; 3. ————; 4. Dawnay. Sinister, Pollard.

Betham, late Ulster King of Arms, states that this Sir John Croker was at Agincourt with Henry V., and distinguished himself by his bravery). They had a son, Sir John Croker, of Lineham,* &c., temp. Edward IV. He married Elizabeth, daughter of Robert Yeo, of Heanton Sachville (*see Yeo*), and died May 8, 1508. He was Cup and Standard Bearer to King Edward IV. *Prince, in his " Worthies of Devon"* says, "As to Sir John Croker, what brought " him first into favour at court, whether courage and skill in arms, " or readiness of address, or what else, I do not find, but he became " so gracious with King Edward IV., that he was admitted his " sworn servant in the honourable office of cupbearer, who, *in " remunerationis servitii, gave a cup d'or, having in the centre a " rose, p.p.r., for the crest unto his coat armour,* and moreover " bestowed upon him the honour of knighthood." This crest was further augmented, in 1475, by Louis XI. of France, with *three fleurs-de-lis, p.p.r.,* on the occasion of Sir John accompanying his master into France. "The addition of the fleurs-de-lis," says Burke, in his "History of the Commoners" (article Croker), "was " one of those attentions on the part of the French monarch, " Louis XI., by which he sought to flatter the vanity and gain the " goodwill of the English gentry." "On ministers," says Hume, " he lavished pensions and pecuniary bribes. To less influential " persons, such lighter, but more honourable favours, as this to " Sir John Croker. The tomb of this Sir John Croker, with his " effigy in brass (see woodcut), is in the parish church of Yeal-" hampton, Devon," with the following inscription:—" Hic jacet " Johannes Croker, miles, quondam Ciphoramis ac Signifer illustris-" simi regis Edwardi quarti, qui obiit Maii 8, anno Domini mille-" simo quingentesimo octavo." The son of this man and Elizabeth Yeo was Sir John Croker,† of Lineham, living temp. Henry VIII., who married, 1st, Elizabeth, daughter of Sir Lewis Pollard,‡ of Roborrow, co. Devon (*see Pollard*); and 2nd, Jane Arundel, but had no issue by her. By his first wife he left a son—

John Croker, of Lineham, who married Elizabath, daughter of Richard Strode,§ of Newnham, Devon (*see Strode*), and by her had—

John Croker, of Lineham, married Agnes, daughter and co-heiress of John Servington, of Tavistock, Devon, and by her had three sons and one daughter. Their eldest son was Hugh Croker, of Lineham, who married Agnes, daughter and co-heiress of John Bonvile, of Ivybridge (*see Bonvile*).

According to Westcote (in his "Devonshire Pedigrees," article Croker), they left four sons and five daughters, of whose offspring

---

* In the Harleian MSS. 889, back of folio 54, this Sir John Croker is called Robert, who married Elizabeth Yeo; but in the Harleian MSS. 5185, back of folio 40, and in the Harleian MSS. 1538, back of folio 104, he is called John. *Risdon,* in his "Survey "of Devon," page 134, makes this Sir John Croker, living in 1497, and who was cupbearer to Edward IV., to have married a Cham-pernown; but this seems clearly wrong, as it transposes all the Croker marriages throughout. He says, ". . . amongst whom " Sir John Croker, Knight, was cupbearer to King Edward IV. ". . . This gentleman married the daughter of Champernown; " his father, the daughter and heir of Bonvile; his grandson, Ser-" vingston's co-heir."

† Prince, in his "Worthies of Devon," says that he was high-sheriff for the county in the first year of Henry VIII.

‡ Through this marriage came the *Delaways,* or *Davies*—a Norman family,—and also the Coplestones (*see Coplestone*).

§ This family still exists in the male line. The present represen-tative, George Strode, Esq., resides at Newnham Park, in the parish of Plympton St. Mary. Through this match came the For-tescues (*see Fortescue*). *Westcote,* in his Croker pedigree, page 550, introduces here, as the issue of this Sir John Croker and Elizabeth Strode, another John Croker, who married Elizabeth, daughter of Robert Yeo, of Heanton Sachville, but this must be the same man who was cupbearer to King Edward IV., Westcote having pro-bably made a mistake in copying the MSS.

---

different accounts are given.* The following is taken from Burke's "History of the Commoners," Vol. IV., article Fox:—

Hugh Croker, of Lineham = Agnes, daughter of Bonville.
married circa 1580

1. John Croker = Joan (1st wife) of Lineham. daughter of — Lee, Esq.

2. Francis Croker = —— married circa 1625.

John Croker, = Jane, daughter of Sir of Lineham. John Pole, and sister of Sir Courtenay Pole.

George Croker = Anstice Tripp, of Yealhamp-ton. of Kings-bridge.

Courtenay Croker = —— of Lineham.

Tabitha Croker = Francis Fox, of St. Germans.

Mary Croker = James Bulteel, of Flete. of Lineham.

NOTE ON THE IRISH FAMILY OF CROKER.

Thomas Croker, of Trevillas, Cornwall, the second son of John Croker, of Lineham, and Elizabeth Strode, married Margery Gill, of Tavistock, and obtained, about 1600, the estate of Ballyanker, in the county of Waterford. He had several sons, and whilst the eldest remained at Trevillas (where his branch is supposed to be extinct), the younger ones, to the number of three or four, migrated to Ireland. They were all probably soldiers; two of them, at least, were so, and distinguished themselves by the extraordinary and almost romantic capture of the city of Waterford in 1650 (*see Smith's "History of Waterford," page 147, edit.* 1774). One of the brothers was killed in the assault, and another (Hugh), after a long course of military service, settled at Ballyanker, and died 1663. From him descended, in seven generations, *the Right Honourable John Wilson Croker, LL.D., F.A.S.* His next brother, Edward Croker, of Rawleighstown, co. Limerick (who was murdered in the Irish rebellion of 1641), was ancestor of the respectable and wealthy family of Croker, of Ballynagarde and Raleighstown, Limerick (at present represented by *Edward Croker, Esq.,* who married,

---

* *Prince, in his "Worthies"* (edit. 1810, *note*), gives a different account of the descendants of Hugh Croker and Agnes Bonvile. It is this:—

Hugh Croker = Agnes Bonvile.

1. John Croker = —— Leigh.
John Croker = —— Pole.
Courtenay Croker = —— Hillesden.

2. Francis Croker = —— Pascoe.
George Croker = Anstice Tripp.
Tabitha Croker = Francis Fox.

Maria Croker = James Bulteel.

The following is taken from Incledon's MSS., formerly in the possession of the late J. H. S. Pigott, Esq., of Brockley, Somerset.

Hugh Croker = Agnes Bonvile.

John Croker, died *s.p.*

Francis Croker = Pascoe, de St. Stevens hæres fratris Johannis juxta Saltash, filia et in Lineham. hæres.

Johannes Croker = Pole, filia Johannis hæres. Pole Baronetti de Shute

Georgius = Anstice Tripp, Croker. filiaNico Tripp, de Kingsbridge

Courtenay Croker = Hillersden

Tabitha Croker = Franciscus Fox, de St. Germans.

Maria Croker = Jacobus Bulteel, de Lineham. de Flete.

1841, Lady Georgina Ellen Monck, sixth daughter of Henry Stanley, Earl of Rathdown, and has a large family), and of a numerous branch settled in Dublin, to which belong *Thomas Crofton Croker, Esq., F.S.A.*, and *Anne*, daughter and heiress of Thomas Croker, Esq., and wife of Sir Edward Crofton, Baronet. She was created, 1797, *Baroness Crofton* in her own right.

Arms and Crest: Same as above.

Motto: " Deus alit eos."

CHURCHILL.

Gitto de Leon, of a noble family in Normandy, living A.D. 1055, had issue, two sons—
　I. Richard de Leon, Lord of Montalban.
　II. Wandril de Leon, Lord of Courcil, from whom is descended the family of Churchill.
He married Isabel de Tuya, and by her had—i. Roger de Courcil; ii. Rowland (ancestor of the Courcils of Picton). " Roger de " Courcil, being one of those who accompanied William, Duke of " Normandy, in his invasion of this realm, A.D. 1066, had, in " reward of his services, divers lands in Somersetshire, Dorsetshire, " and Devonshire (as appears by Doomsday Book), among which " was the Lordship of Churchill, in the county of Somerset, the " place of his abode, and from which he took his surname, being " written in the old records Curichil, Cheuchill, Chirchil, &c."
He married Gertrude, daughter of Sir Guy de Torbay, and by her had—
John de Chirchil, who married Joan de Kilrington, and by her had—
Sir Bartholomew de Chirchil. He held the Castle of Bristol for King Stephen.
He married Agnes, daughter of Sir Ralph FitzRalph, Lord of Tiverton, Devon, and had—
Pagan de Cherchill, who also left a son—
Roger de Cherchill, living in the time of Edward I. His son was—
Elias de Cherchelle. He married Dorothy, daughter of the ancient family of Columbers, and by her had three sons; viz.—
　1. John Churchill, married Joan Dawney, and left two daughters:—i. Margaret, married Andrew Hibbersden; ii. Agnes, married Thomas Gifford, whereby the Lordship of Churchill, and other lands devolved upon them.
　2. Giles Churchill. He held the Lordship of Yealhampton and Lineham, co. Devon, and had one daughter, Agnes Churchill, who married Sir John Croker (*see Croker*), and carried these estates into his family.
　3. William Churchill, of Rockbear, co. Devon. The family of *Churchill, Duke of Marlborough*, spring from this third son, through eight generations, to Sir Winston Churchill, born 1620.

Arms: Sable; a lion rampant, argent; over all a bendlet dexter gules.

Crest: A demi-lion rampant, argent.

Taken from Collins' Peerage, edition 1812, by Sir Egerton Brydges, Vol. I., p. 362.

POLLARD.

Walter Pollard, of Horwood, in the county of Devon, lived in the twenty-seventh year of Henry III. " After that, another " Walter, in the twenty-fourth year of Edward I.; then Joel; then " John, who married Emma, daughter and co-heir of Sir John " Doddiscombe, and had issue, Walter, who married Elizabeth, " daughter and co-heir of William Cornu, and had issue, John, " who married Eleanor Coplestone, daughter of John Coplestone, " of Coplestone (*see Coplestone*), and had issue, Walter, and

" Robert, who married Agnes Lewknor, daughter of Lewknor, of " Sussex." Their son was Lewis Pollard, 1465-1540, one of the Justices of the Common Pleas in the reign of Henry VIII., married Agnes Hext, of Kingston, near Totness, Devon, and left a very numerous family, " amongst whom were Hugh Richard, John " Robert, Anthony, *Elizabeth, who married Sir John Croker,* " *of Lineham, co. Devon* (*see Croker*); Jane, Agnes, Thomasin, " and Philippa."

Arms: Argent ; a chevron sable, between three escalops gules.

Taken from Prince's " Worthies of Devon," and Westcote's " Devonshire Pedigrees," article Pollard.

YEO.

Nicholas Yeo, of Heanton Sachville = Elizabeth, daughter and heir of
　　　　　　　　　　　　　　　　　　　　Sachville.

　John Yeo = Alice

William Yeo = Anne, daughter and heir of John Esse, or Ash, of
　　　　　　　　Westesse.

　Robert Yeo = Joan, daughter and heir of William Pyne, of
　　　　　　　　Bradwell.

　Robert Yeo = Isabell, daughter and heir of John Brightly, of
　　　　　　　　Brightly.

　John Yeo = Alice, daughter and co-heir of William Jew, of
　　　　　　　Cotleigh.

　William Yeo = Ellen, daughter and co-heir of William Grenvil, of
　　　　　　　　Stow, in Cornwall.

　　Robert Yeo = Alice, daughter of John Walrond, of Bradfield.

Philip, William, Nicholas, Edward, Robert, *Elisabeth* Yeo = *John Croker, of Lineham* (*see Croker*).

Arms: Argent; a chevron sable between three drakes azure, beak and legs or.

Crest: A peacock close, p.p.r.

Taken from John Tuckett's " Devonshire Pedigrees," recorded in the Herald's Visitation of 1620.

COPLESTONE.

Prince says, " When this family first grew eminent I do not find, " but if common tradition holds true, it flourished in these parts " before the Conquest. However, if so, it was eclipsed as most of " the Saxon race were, a long while by the interposition of the " Norman Conqueror; for Sir William Pole tells us he had not " found any of this name until the days of King Edward II., in " which William de Coplestone was set down as a witness to a " deed, and also Richard Coplestone, of Coplestone. Which " Richard had issue, Adam, who had issue, John, who, by " Katherine his wife, daughter and heir of John Graas, of Ting " Graas, had issue, John Coplestone, of Coplestone, who, by " Elizabeth his wife, daughter and heir of John Hawly, of Dart- " mouth, had issue, Philip, John, Walter, and *Eleanor Coplestone,* " *married to John Pollard, Esq., of Horwood, co. Devon*" (*see Pollard*).

[Note.—They were wont to be styled *Coplestone, the " White Spur."* This office was made by creation of the king, the ceremony whereof was thus:—What gentleman the king was pleased to bestow this honour upon, he was wont to put about his neck a silver collar of esses, or SSS, and to confer upon him a pair of silver spurs. Whereupon, in the west part of the kingdom, they be called *White Spurs*, by which they are distinguished from knights, who are wont to wear gilt spurs. The title of White Spur was hereditary, and always belonged only to the heir male of the family. —*Prince.*]

Arms : Argent ; a chevron engrailed gules, between three leopards' faces azure, two and one.

Crest : A demi-griffin, salient gules, armed or without wings.

Taken from Prince's " Worthies of Devon," and Westcote's "Devonshire Pedigrees," article Coplestone ; and also from Tuckett's " Devonshire Pedigrees."

STRODE.

The first of the name was Adam Strode, of Strode, in the parish of Ermington, near Modbury, co. Devon, at which place he resided in the time of King Henry III. There successively followed this Adam Strode, Roger Strode, Richard Strode, William Strode, John Strode, and Reginald Strode, who, by Florence his wife, had issue, John Strode, of Strode, who married Melior, daughter of William Solman, and had issue, John Strode, who, by Jane, daughter of Burleigh, of Clanacomb, in the parish of Modbury, had issue, Richard Strode. He married *Margaret, daughter of Henry Fortescue, of Wood (see Fortescue)*, and had two sons—1st. William, d.*s.p.* ; 2nd. Richard Strode, who, by Joan, his wife, daughter and heir of Ellis Penilles, of Plympton, had issue, Richard, who, by Agnes, daughter of John Milliton, of Mewy, had issue, William, Francis, and Richard, and two daughters—1st. Cicely, married Thomas Fortescue, of Winston ; and 2nd. *Elizabeth Strode, married to John Croker, of Lineham (see Croker).*

Arms : Argent ; a chevron, between three conies passant, sable.

Crest : On a mount, a savin tree vert, fructed gules.

Taken from Prince's " Worthies of Devon," and Westcote's and Tuckett's " Devonshire Pedigrees," article Strode.

FORTESCUE.

Sir Richard le Forte fought under William the Conqueror at the Battle of Hastings, whence he obtained for himself and posterity the name of Fortescue. His son was Sir Adam Fortescue, who obtained Wymondeston, or Wynston, in the parish of Modbury, co. Devon. His son was John Fortescue, who received a confirmation of the lands from King John. The succession assigned by Sir William Pole is from this John Fortescue, through Robert, three Adams, and William, to William, who married the heiress of Beauchamp. He had two sons—1st. William Fortescue, of Wynston ; and 2nd. Sir John Fortescue (*Captain of Meaux*), who, by his wife, daughter and heiress of Norreis, of Norreis, had three sons

—1st. Sir Henry Fortescue, of Fallopit and Wood (Chief Justice of Ireland). His descendant, *Margaret, married Richard Strode (see Strode)*; 2nd. Richard Fortescue, of Pulesborn ; 3rd. Sir John Fortescue, the Chancellor of England.

Arms : Azure ; a bend engrailed argent, cotised or.

Crest : An heraldic tiger passant, argent ; armed, maned, and tufted or.

Motto : " Forte scutum solus ducum."

Taken from Westcote's " Devonshire Pedigrees," Prince's " Worthies of Devon," edit. 1810, with the note at the end of the article Fortescue.

BONVILE.

" Sir Nicholas Bonvile, of Wiscombe (in the parish of Southlegh, " co. Devon). married Amesia, and had issue, Sir William Bonvile, " Knight, which, by Joan, his wife, had issue, Nicholas, which, by " Matilda, his wife [daughter and co-heir of Sir Thomas Pine, of " Shute, of the same family with Sir Adrian du Pin, one of the " Knights of the Round Table, of King Arthur's institution, " about the year of our Lord 520], had issue, Sir Nicholas Bonvile, " Knight, which, by Margaret [daughter and co-heiress of Sir " William Damarel, of Woodbury, Devon], had issue, John and " others. John Bonvile died in the lifetime of his father, but by " Elizabeth, Lady of Chuton, had issue, William,* Lord Bonvile " [who was beheaded after the second battle of St. Albans]. He " married Margaret Meriet, and had issue, Sir William Bonvile, " which died in the lifetime of his father, but left issue, by Eliza- " beth, his wife [the only daughter and heiress of William, Lord " Harrington], William Bonvile, Lord Harrington, which also died " in the lifetime of his grandfather, but left issue, by Catherine, " one of the daughters of William Nevil, Earl of Salisbury, Cicely, " his only child, who afterwards brought a vast estate to Thomas " Grey, Earl of Dorset."

Arms : Sable ; six mullets argent, pierced gules, three, two, and one.

Taken from Prince's " Worthies of Devon," article Bonvile.

---

* " William, Lord Bonvile, by Elizabeth Kirkby, left a natural " son, called John Bonvile, on whom he settled his estate at Ivy " Bridge ; but he, having no male issue, left Ivy Bridge to John " Bonvile, his natural son, whose name, after three generations, " expired in a daughter and heiress, married unto Hugh Croker, of " Lineham " (*see Croker*).

ADDENDA.

Mary, daughter of John Petty Dearman (*see* page 16), married 22 March, 1819, to George Braithwaite Lloyd, of Birmingham, who married, 2ndly, Mary Shipton, and died 6 November, 1857. She died 16 August, 1826, having had two sons and two daughters.

(1.) Sampson Samuel Lloyd, Esq., of Moor Hall, Sutton Coldfields, co. Warwick, married 1st, Emma, daughter of Samuel and Mary Reeve, and has issue—
1. Sampson Samuel Lloyd, married 4 August, 1868, Jane Emilia, daughter of Thomas Lloyd, Esq., of the Priory, Warwick, and has a son, Charles Sampson Llewellyn Lloyd, born 2 June, 1869.
2. George Hubert ; 3. Arther Llewellyn.

1. Emma Mary Lloyd, married to James Johnston, Captain H.M. Indian Army.
2. Mary Dearman ; 3. Rachel Louisa ; 4. Priscilla Caroline ; 5. Alice Elizabeth ; and 6. Adelaide Beatrice Lloyd.
Sampson Samuel Lloyd married, 2ndly, at Bückeburn, Northern Germany, 11 October, 1865, Marie Wilhelmine Sophie Christiane Menckhoff, daughter of His Excellency William Frederick Menckhoff, Lieut.-General in the Prussian army, and has two sons, Charles Frederick Lloyd, and Walter Reginald Lloyd.
(2.) George Braithwaite Lloyd, Esq., of the Grove, Edgbaston, married Mary Hutchinson, of Sunderland, and has an only son, John Henry Lloyd, born 14 April, 1855.
(1.) Priscilla Caroline ; and (2.) Mary Lloyd ; both died young.

List of Matches.

Abbott, Elizabeth, and Charles Prideaux, 17.
Abrahams, Melita, and Henry T. Fox, 13.
Aitkins, Margaret, and George F. B. Mewburn, 7.
Alexander, Catherine, and Thomas Fox, 9.
   ,,   Hannah, and Edward Fox, 9.
Allen, Elizabeth, and William Southall, 13.
   ,,   Frances, and Nathaniel Tregelles, 13.
   ,,   John, and Elizabeth Fox, 13.
   ,,   ,,   Elizabeth Wright, 13.
   ,,   ,,   Frances Fox, 8, 13.
   ,,   Mary, and John Eliott, 13.
   ,,   Pearson, and Maria Churchill, 11.
   ,,   Rebecca, and William Matthews, 13.
Angell, Sarah, and Joseph John Fox, 13.
Anstice, Mary C., and William Prideaux, 17.
Applebee, Lovall, and John Fox, 7.
Ayre, William, and Mary T. McDonald, 7.
Backhouse, M.P., Edmund, and Juliet Mary Fox, 11.
   ,,   Jane Gurney, and Robert B. Fox, 11.
   ,,   Jonathan E., and Florence Trelawny, 11.
Ball, Fanny, and Frederick Prideaux, 18.
   ,,   Francis C., and Emily B. Prideaux, 18.
   ,,   Sarah, and Joseph Hingston, 18.
Barclay, Lucy, and George Croker Fox, 11.
   ,,   Mary, and Robert Were Fox, 11.
Baskerville, Louisa, and Thomas W. McDonald, 7.
Bassett, Ellen Mary, and Robert Fox, 11.
Bathurst, ———, and Charles Wethered, 22.
Bawden, Anna, and Charles Bawden, 20.
   ,,   Charles, and Anna Bawden, 20.
   ,,   Esther, and Philip C. Prideaux, 17, 20.
   ,,   Jonathan, and Anna Tuckett, 20.
Bayley, Elizabeth S., and Rev. U. Cookworthy, 18.
Bealing, Mary, and George Fox, 6.
Berry, Eleanor, and ——— Hemming, 6.
   ,,   Lydia, and John Fox, 7.
   ,,   Nicholas, and Mary Elliott, 6.
Best, Henry W., and Emily de Horne, 17.
Beswick, Hannah, and John Tuckett, 20.
Bevan, Edward, and Maria Goodwin, 8.
   ,,   Mary, and Alfred Waterhouse, 8.
   ,,   Paul, and Rebecca Capper, 8.
   ,,   ,,   Judith N. Dillwyn, 8.
   ,,   Samuel, and Caroline Brooks, 8.
   ,,   Sylvanus, and Mary Fox, 8.
   ,,   William, and Marie S. Read, 8.
Bevington, Alexander, and Louisa de Horne, 17.
   ,,   George, and Katharine Collier de Horne, 17.
   ,,   Katherine C., and Alfred Christy, 17.
Binns, Frances, and Nicholas Were, 20.
   ,,   Jonah, and Abigail Tuckett, 20.
   ,,   Jonathan, and Anna Debell, 20.
   ,,   Thomas, and Rachel Sparkes, 20.
Birdwood, Ann, and James Fox, 15.

Birkbeck, Sarah, and Francis Fox, 11.
Blaker, Eliza, and Arthur B. Collier, 16.
Blater, Judith, and Joseph Ellicot, 22.
Blewett, Sarah, and George de Horne, 17.
Bond, H. M., and Evan T. Ellicot, 22.
Botters, Rachel, and Philip Cookworthy, 18, 19.
   ,,   William, and Rachel Debell, 19.
Bracher, Hannah, and John Tuckett, 20.
Bradley, Eliza de France, and W. H. Chapline, 20.
Braithwaite, Mary, and Charles Hingston, M.D., 19.
Broadrick, Richard F., R.N., and Frances M. Crewdson, 8.
Brooke, Elizabeth, and George Ellicot, 23.
Brooking, Amy, and Benjamin Debell, 19.
Brooks, Caroline, and Samuel Bevan, 8.
Brown, Catherine, and Edward Long Fox, 14.
   ,,   Elizabeth, and Andrew Ellicot, 22.
   ,,   Esther, and Andrew Ellicot, 22.
   ,,   Leah, and John Ellicot, 23.
   ,,   Mary, and Edward Fox, 10.
   ,,   Sarah, and Andrew Ellicot, 22.
Browne, William, and Catharine T. Hingston, 19.
Bruce, Thomas, and Anne Fox, 6.
Buckham, Mary A., and Dillworth C. Fox, 9.
Buckingham, Anne, and Samuel Churchill, 11.
Bulgin, Martha, and Elias H. Tuckett, 20.
Bull, James, and Josephine Fox, 11.
Burges, Mary Janet, and William Waterhouse, 8.
Burnand, Louisa, and John W. Janson, 16.
Bush, Mary, and James Fox, 15.
Bussell, J. G., and Charlotte Cookworthy, 18.
Butler, Eliza, and Abraham de Horne, 17.
Bye, Ann, and Andrew Ellicot, 22.
Cadbury, Anna, and Samuel Churchill, 11.
   ,,   Joel, and Sarah Fox, 11.
   ,,   John, and Anna ———, 11.
Calmady, Cycill C., and William F. Collier, 16.
Capper, Rebecca, and Paul Bevan, 8.
Carey, Hannah, and William E. Coale, 23.
   ,,   James, and Martha Ellicot, 23.
   ,,   John Ellicot, and ——— Irvine, 23.
   ,,   Margaret, and Galloway Cheston, 23.
   ,,   Martha, and Dr. Thomas, 23.
   ,,   Samuel, and ——— Evans, 23.
   ,,   Thomas, and Martha Leiper, 23.
Cartwright, Frederick Fox, and Katherine L. F. Danger, 15.
   ,,   George Leopold, and Anna Mary Fox, 15.
Champion, Esther, and Philip D. Tuckett, 20.
   ,,   Sarah, and Charles Fox, 7.
Chapline, Alexander H., and Dorcas J. Dorsey, 20.
   ,,   Elizabeth G , and Percival M. Potts, 21.
   ,,   Jane Ralph, and Robert Stanton, 21.
   ,,   Josephine Isabella, and Thomas B. Roby, 21.
   ,,   Maria Louise, and Jonathan C. Lawrence, 21.
   ,,   Mary Ann, and Josiah W. Pomeroy, 20.

Chapline, Mary A. Pomeroy, and Samuel P. Norton, 20.
  ,,   Moses W., and Elizabeth Miller Fox, 20.
  ,,   ,,   ,,   Margaret S. Thomas, 20.
  ,,   Rowena C., and Charles P. Robbins, 21.
  ,,   Sophia Jane, and Alphonso F. Tilden, 21.
  ,,   William Henry, and Eliza de France Bradley, 20.
Chapman, Caroline, and Charles H. Fox, 9.
Charleton, James, and Elizabeth Fox, 9.
  ,,   Robert, and Catherine B. Fox, 9.
Charsley, William Henry, and Eliza M. J. Fox, 12.
Cheston, Galloway, and Margaret Carey, 23.
Chetwynd, Harriet C., and A. de Horne Christy, 17.
Christy, Alfred, and Katherine C. Bevington, *née* de Horne, 17.
  ,,   Arthur de Horne, and Harriet C. Chetwynd, 17.
  ,,   Edward, and Julia Shears Spurrell, 17.
  ,,   Emma C. Collier, and Geo. Steinman Steinman, 17.
  ,,   Frederick Collier, and Caroline Wells, 17.
  ,,   John, and Sarah de Horne, 17.
  ,,   John de Horne, and Ann Kidder, 17.
Churchill, Maria, and Pearson Allen, 11.
  ,,   Samuel, and Anna Cadbury, 11.
  ,,   ,,   Anne Buckingham, 11.
Clark, Deborah, and John Lawrence Hinton, 15.
  ,,   Jane Applebee, and Alfred Hinton, 15.
  ,,   Thomas Baskerville, and Elizabeth Mason, 15.
  ,,   William, and Jane Fox, 15.
Cloak, Mary, and Joshua Hancock, 6.
  ,,   Peter, and Mary Fox, 6.
Coale, William E., and Hannah Carey, 23.
Coffin, Mary Desmond, and Washington Fox, 14.
Cogger, Mary, and Francis Fox, 6.
Collier, Amy, and Joseph Pike, 16.
  ,,   Arthur Bevan, and Eliza Blaker, 16.
  ,,   Benjamin, and Katharine Reynolds, 16.
  ,,   Charlotte, and Edward James, 16.
  ,,   Elizabeth Anna, and Col. Jas. K. Pipon, 16.
  ,,   Harriet, and Wm. Freeman, 16.
  ,,   John, and Anna Debell, 16.
  ,,   ,,   Martha Padley, 16.
  ,,   ,,   Emma Porrett, 16.
  ,,   John Francis, and Frances A. J. Jenner, 16.
  ,,   Joseph, and Dorothy Fox, 7, 16.
  ,,   ,,   Mary Elworthy, 16.
  ,,   Mary, and Abraham de Horne, 16.
  ,,   Mortimer John, and Mary Elizabeth Harris, 16.
  ,,   ,,   ,,   Sophy L. Whipple, 16.
  ,,   Rachel, and John Hingston, 16, 18.
  ,,   Rt. Hon. Sir Robert, and Isabella Rose Rose, 16.
  ,,   Sarah, and Benjamin Cookworthy, 16, 18.
  ,,   William, and Mary Hingston, 16.
  ,,   William Fredk., and Cycill C. Calmady, 16.
Collins, George Samuel, and Julia A. Prideaux, 18.
Cook, Hannah, and Henry F. Pickering, 21.
Cooke, Rev. Edward W., and Adeline Fox, 12.
Cookworthy, Anna, and George Prideaux, 17, 18.
  ,,   Benjamin, and Sarah Collier, 18.
  ,,   Charlotte, and J. G. Bussell, 18.
  ,,   Edith, and Rev. A. P. Sanderson, 18.
  ,,   Frederick, and Sarah Ring, 18.
  ,,   ,,   Mary C. Cookworthy, 18.
  ,,   Jacob, and Sarah Morris, 18.
  ,,   John, and Charlotte Spicer, 18.
  ,,   Joseph, and Rebecca Fox, 15, 18.
  ,,   ,,   Mary Robins, 18.
  ,,   Joseph Collier, and Jane Urquhart, 18.
  ,,   ,,   ,,   ——— Lugger, 18.
  ,,   Mary Collier, and Fredk. Cookworthy, 18.
  ,,   Mary Frances, and Thomas Webster, Q.C., 18.
  ,,   Philip, and Rachel Botters, 18.
  ,,   Sarah, and Francis Fox, 11, 18.

Cookworthy, Susanna, and Joseph Debell, 19.
  ,,   William, and Edith Debell, 18, 19.
  ,,   William (*née* Fox), and Tabitha Fox, 8, 11.
  ,,   Capt. William S., and Emily Ellen Graham, 18.
  ,,   Rev. Urquhart, and Elizabeth S. Bayley, 18.
Cooper, Esther, and Charles James Fox, 15.
Cope, Isaac G., and Elizabeth C. Dungan, 21.
Coppock, Rebecca J., and Josiah F. Pickering, 21.
Cosserat, Elizabeth, and William Fox, 12.
Cox, Elizabeth, and Nathaniel Fox, 13.
Crawley, Emma, and Edward Matravers, 8.
Crewdson, Ellen Fox, and Frederick Wadsworth, 8.
  ,,   Frances E., and Richard R. Fox, 10.
  ,,   Frances Mary, and Richard Fletcher Broadrick, R.N., 8.
  ,,   Rev. George, and Mary Salome Hay Sweet Escott, 7.
  ,,   George Braithwaite, and Eleanor Fox, 7.
  ,,   Maria, and Francis E. Fox, 10.
  ,,   Rachel, and Henry Fox, 9.
  ,,   Sarah, and Charles Fox, 9.
  ,,   Thomas, and Jane Fox, 8.
  ,,   William Dillworth, and Sarah Fox, 14.
  ,,   ,,   ,,   Katherine Davidson, 7.
  ,,   Wilson, and Ellen Waterhouse, 8.
Croker, Samuel, and Deborah Fox, 6.
  ,,   Tabitha, and Francis Fox, 6.
Cross, William, and Caroline Tuckett, 20.
Crouch, Edward Anson, and Mary Fox, 7.
  ,,   Frances Anne, and James Grace, 7.
Curtis, George Douglas, and Cynthia Anna Riggs, 21.
  ,,   Helen, and Alfred Tuckett, 20.
  ,,   Josiah Fox, and Landorria Lorentz, 21.
  ,,   Mary, and Wylie H. Oldham, 21.
  ,,   Robert J., and Anna Applebee Fox, 21.
Danger, Katherine Long Fox, and Fredk. Fox Cartwright, 15.
  ,,   Thomas, and Katherine Long Fox, 15.
  ,,   ,,   Louisa Caroline Fox, 15.
Davidson, Katherine, and William Dillworth Crewdson, 7.
Davis, Henry, and Jane B. Fox, 14.
  ,,   ——— and Joanna E. Fox, 11.
  ,,   Maria, and ——— Motte, 14.
  ,,   Mary E., and Ernest A. Hingston, 19.
Dearman, Eliza Jane, and William Janson, 16.
  ,,   John Petty, and Priscilla Fox, 15.
  ,,   Mary, and George Braithwaite Lloyd, 16.
Debell, Anna and George Fox, 11, 19.
  ,,   ,,   Jonathan Binns, 20.
  ,,   ,,   John Collier, 16.
  ,,   ,,   James Tuckett, 19, 20.
  ,,   Benj., and Amy Brooking, 19.
  ,,   Edith, and William Cookworthy, 19.
  ,,   ,,   Wm. Hancock, 19.
  ,,   John, and Mary ———, 19.
  ,,   ,,   Mary Stephens, 19.
  ,,   Joseph, and Margaret Diamond, 19,
  ,,   ,,   Susannah Cookworthy, 19.
  ,,   Mary, and James Tuckett, 19, 20.
  ,,   ,,   Joseph Tregelles, 19.
  ,,   Philip, and ——— Wilmoth, 19.
  ,,   ,,   Anna Soady, 19.
  ,,   ,,   Sarah Fox, 7, 19.
  ,,   Rachel, and Wm. Botters, 19.
  ,,   Robert, and Mary Peake, 19.
  ,,   ,,   Grace Williams, 19.
  ,,   Sarah, and Richard Wadge, 19.
  ,,   Wilmoth, and John Read, 19.
Derry, Rebecca, and James Rice, 6.
Dewing, Reginald, and Rosette Hingston, 19.
Diamond, Margaret, and Joseph Debell, 19.
Dillwyn, Judith N., and Paul Bevan, 8.
Dobree, Jane, and George Smith Fox, 9.

Dorsey, Dorcas J., and Alexander H. Chapline, 20.
Doyle, Emily Anne, and Dr. Wilson Fox, 9.
Dungan, Benj. Ellis, and Sarah S. Fox, 21.
,, Charles James, and Susan G. Lemmon, 21.
,, Elizabeth Chapline, and Isaac G. Cope, 21.
,, Julia Updegraff, and John A. Leash, 22.
Dymond, Robert, and Josephine Hingston, 18.
Edmunds, Anna, and Philip D. Tuckett, 20.
Eliott, Elizabeth, and Silvanus James, 13.
,, John, and Mary Allen, 13.
,, ,, Mary Ann Sturge, 13.
,, Joseph, and Alice Thompson, 13.
,, Samuel, and Jane Mann, 13.
Ellicot, Andrew, and Elizabeth Brown, 22.
,, ,, Esther ,, 22.
,, ,, Sarah ,, 22.
,, ,, Ann Bye, 22.
,, ,, Mary Fox, 7, 22.
,, ,, Emily McFadon, 22.
,, ,, Hannah Tunis, 22.
,, Anna, and Thomas Tyson, 23.
,, Elias, and Mary Thomas, 22.
,, Elizabeth, and William E. George, 22.
,, ,, Thomas Lee, 23.
,, ,, Lewin Wethered, 22.
,, ,, Nathaniel Ellicot, 23.
,, Evan T., and H. M. Bond, 22.
,, George, and Elizabeth Brooke, 23.
,, James, and H. Thomas, 22.
,, John, and Leah Brown, 23.
,, ,, Cassender Hopkinson, 23.
,, ,, Mary Mitchell, 23.
,, Jonathan, and Sarah Harvey, 22.
,, Joseph, and Judith Blater, 22.
,, Letitia, and John Evans, 22.
,, Martha, and James Carey, 23.
,, ,, Nathan Tyson, 23.
,, Mary, and Nicholas Emmett, 22.
,, ,, Thomas Tyson, 23.
,, Nathaniel, and Elizabeth Ellicot, 23.
,, Rachel, and John Hewes, 22.
,, Samuel, and Mary Ann Todhunter, 22.
,, Sarah, and William Tyson, 22.
,, Tacy, and Joseph King, 22.
,, ,, Isaac Macpherson, 22.
,, Thomas, and Ann Ely, 23.
,, ,, Louis McFadon, 22.
,, ,, Mary Miller, 22.
,, William, and —— Pulteney, 22.
Elliott, Mary, and Nicholas Berry, 6.
,, ,, Nathaniel Ford, 6.
,, ,, John Rice, 6.
,, Nicholas and Mary Fox, 6.
,, ,, Honor Hinds, 6.
Elworthy, Mary, and Joseph Fox, 16.
Ely, Ann, and Thomas Ellicot, 23.
Emmett, Elizabeth, and Clement Jackson, 22.
,, Mary, and Benjamin Fox, 7.
,, Nicholas, and Mary Ellicot, 22.
Enoch, William, and Lucy Jackson, 22.
Escott, Mary Salome H. S., and Rev. George Crewdson, 7.
Evans, John, and Letitia Ellicot, 22.
,, Wm., and Mary Randall, 22.
,, —— and Samuel Carey, 23.
Ferrier, Hannah, and Charles Fox, 15.
Festing, Captain Henry, and Sarah de Horne, 17.
Flannering, Joanna, and Joshua Fox, 11.
Folle, J., and Elizabeth Hancock, 20.
Foot, Henry B., and Sophia Fox, 10.
Ford, Mary, and Edward Richards, 6.

Ford, Nathaniel, and Mary Elliott, 6.
Forster, Hannah, and Richard Fox, 13.
Fortescue, Jane, and Francis Fox, 15.
Fothergill, Mary, and William Tuckett, 20.
Fowler, Robert N., M.P., and Sarah C. Fox, 12.
,, William, M.P., and Elizabeth F. Tuckett, 20.
Fox, Adeline, and Rev. Edward Wilson Cooke, 12.
,, Alexander, and Ellen Phillips, 13.
,, Alfred, and Sarah Lloyd, 12.
,, Alfred Lloyd, and Mary Jane Fox, 10, 12.
,, Anna, and Frederick Hingston Fox, 9, 10.
,, ,, John Sanderson, 9.
,, ,, William Rawes, 13.
,, Anna Applebee, and Robert J. Curtis, 21.
,, Anna Mary, and Rev. George L. Cartwright, 15.
,, Anna Rebecca, and Edward B. Tylor, 9.
,, Anne, and Thomas Bruce, 6.
,, ,, John Gwin, 6.
,, Benjamin, and Mary Emmett, 7.
,, ,, Elizabeth Higman, 7.
,, ,, Sarah Treffry, 7.
,, Berry, and Elizabeth Were, 7.
,, Catherine, and J. Morehead, 10.
,, Catherine Brewster, and Robert Charleton, 9.
,, Charles, and Sarah Champion, 7.
,, ,, Sarah Crewdson, 9.
,, ,, Hannah Ferrier, 15.
,, ,, Margaret Jewell, 7.
,, ,, Sarah Hustler, 11.
,, Charles Henry, and Caroline Chapman, 9.
,, Charles James, and Esther Cooper, 15.
,, ,, ,, Anna M. Kerswill, 7.
,, ,, ,, Amelia Pitt, 12.
,, Charles Joseph, and Ellen Lucas, 14.
,, Charlotte, and Samuel Fox, 9, 11.
,, ,, Joseph James Sessions, 10.
,, Constance Catherine, and Charles H. Tawney, 14.
,, Cornelius, and Emma Jarvis, 7.
,, Cornelius Willes, and Sophia E. Treloar, 7.
,, Deborah, and Samuel Croker, 6.
,, Dillworth Crewdson, and Mary A. Buckham, 9.
,, Dorothy, and Joseph Collier, 7, 16.
,, Edward, and Hannah Alexander, 9.
,, ,, Mary Brown, 10.
,, ,, Johannah Menhennit, 10.
,, ,, Anna Were, 7.
,, Edward Long, and Catherine Brown, 14.
,, ,, ,, Isabella Ker, 14.
,, Edwin, and Margaret Wylie, 10.
,, Edwin Fydell, and Elizabeth A. Pigott, 14.
,, ,, ,, Ellen E. Warrington, 14.
,, Eleanor, and George Braithwaite Crewdson, 7.
,, Eliza Mary Jane, and William Henry Charsley, 12.
,, Elizabeth, and John Allen, 13.
,, ,, James Charleton, 9.
,, ,, William Matravers, 8.
,, Elizabeth Anne, and William Goodeve, 15.
,, Elizabeth Miller, and Moses W. Chapline, 20.
,, Elizabeth Treffry, and Henry W. Taylor, 7.
,, Elizabeth Tregelles, and William Gibbins, 11.
,, Emma, and Joseph Peirce, 10.
,, Frances, and John Allen, 8 and 13.
,, Francis, and Sarah Birkbeck, 11
,, ,, Mary Cogger, 6.
,, ,, Sarah Cookworthy, 11, 18.
,, ,, Tabitha Croker, 6.
,, ,, Jane Fortescue, 15.
,, ,, Charlotte Jackson, 10.
,, ,, Dorothy Kekewich, 6.
,, ,, Hester Mills, 13.

Fox, Francis and Anne Sansom, 7.
,,   ,,   Hannah Scantlebury, 6.
,,   ,,   Joan Smith, 6.
,,   ,,   Rachel Womersley, 10.
,, Francis Drake, and Julianna E. Jennings, 15.
,,   ,,   ,,   Julianna Updegraff, 15.
,, Francis Edward, and Maria Crewdson, 10.
,, Frederick Hingston, and Anna Fox, 9, 10.
,, George, and Mary Bealing, 6.
,,   ,,   Anna Debell, 11, 19.
,,   ,,   Rachel Collier Hingston, 10, 19.
,,   ,,   Frances James, 7.
,,   ,,   Eleanor Rawes, 7.
,,   ,,   Elizabeth Were, 7.
,, George Croker, and Lucy Barclay, 11.
,,   ,,   ,,   Ada Mary Wake, 11.
,,   ,,   ,,   Mary Were, 11.
,,   ,,   ,,   Catherine Young, 11.
,, George Edward, and Jane W. Richardson, 10.
,, George Frederic, and Sarah Anne Newsom, 10.
,, George Frederick, and Ellin Simpson, 14.
,, George Smith, and Jane Dobree, 9.
,, Hannah, and Henry Mewburn, 7.
,, Helen Maria, and Jno. Wm. Pease, 12.
,, Henrietta Maria, and Robert Luke Howard, 9.
,, Henry, and Rachel Crewdson, 9.
,,   ,,   Mary Charlotte Russell, 11.
,, Henry Hawes, and Harriet Jones, 14.
,,   ,,   Elizabeth Gilbert, 14.
,, Henry Treffry, and Fanny Stephens, 7.
,, Henry Tregelles, and Melita Abrahams, 13.
,, Howard, and Olivia Blanche Orme, 12.
,, James, and Ann Birdwood, 15.
,,   ,,   Mary Bush, 15.
,,   ,,   Maria Grigg, 15.
,,   ,,   Elizabeth Record, 6.
,, Jane, and William Clark, 15.
,,   ,,   Thomas Crewdson, 8.
,,   ,,   Thomas Wallis McDonald, 7.
,, Jane Brown, and Henry Davis, 14.
,, Joanna Ellen, and Rev. —— Davis, 11.
,, John, and Lovall Applebee, 7.
,,   ,,   Lydia Berry, 7.
,,   ,,   Rebecca Steevens, 15.
,, John Hingston, and Frances Jackson, 10.
,, Joseph, and Elizabeth Hingston, 12.
,,   ,,   Elizabeth Peters, 12, 13.
,,   ,,   Anne P. Tregelles, 13, 19.
,, Joseph Hingston, and Sarah Elizabeth Tregelles, 10.
,, Joseph Hoyland, and Mariana Fox Tuckett, 9, 20.
,, Joseph John, and Sarah Angell, 13.
,, Joseph Scantlebury, and Jane Lewes Willes, 7.
,, Josephine, and James Bull, 11.
,, Joshua, and Joanna Flannering, 11.
,, Josiah, and Anna Miller, 15.
,, Juliet Mary, and Edmund Backhouse, M.P., 11.
,, Katherine Long, and Thomas Danger, 15.
,, Louisa Caroline, and Thomas Danger, 15.
,, Louisa Mary, and George S. Kiernan, 15.
,, Lucy Anna, and Thomas Hodgkin, 12.
,, Lydia, and John Prideaux, 15.
,, Mariana, and Francis Tuckett, 11, 20.
,, Mary, and Sylvanus Bevan, 8.
,,   ,,   Peter Cloak, 6.
,,   ,,   Edward Anson Crouch, 7.
,,   ,,   Andrew Ellicot, 7, 22.
,,   ,,   Nicholas Elliott, 6.
,,   ,,   Joseph Whitwell Pease, M.P., 12.
,, Mary Brown, and Charles L. Muller, 14.
,, Mary Jane, and Alfred Lloyd Fox, 10, 12.

Fox, Nathaniel, and Elizabeth Cox, 13.
,, Octavius A., and Miriam Simmonds, 10.
,, Philip, and Isabella Ormiston, 12.
,, Philip Browne, and Helen Patterson, 10.
,, Priscilla, and John Petty Dearman, 15.
,, Rachel, and George Hodge, 6.
,,   ,,   John Hingston, 11, 18.
,, Rachel Anna, and Henry B. Gibbins, 10.
,, Rachel Crewdson, and John Edward Wakefield, 9.
,, Rachel Elizabeth, and Saml. Lindoe Fox, 9, 12.
,,   ,,   ,,   Philip D. Tuckett, 12, 20.
,, Rebecca, and Joseph Cookworthy, 15, 18.
,, Rebecca Stevens, and E. Pickering, 21.
,, Richard, and Hannah Forster, 13.
,, Richard Reynolds, and Frances E. Crewdson, 10.
,, Robert, and Ellen Mary Bassett, 11.
,, Robert Barclay, and Jane Gurney Backhouse, 11.
,, Robert Phillips, and Sarah Prideaux, 8.
,, Robert Were, and Mary Barclay, 11.
,,   ,,   ,,   Dorothy Hingston, 10, 18.
,,   ,,   ,,   Rachel C. Prideaux, 10, 18.
,,   ,,   ,,   Sarah Sturge, 10.
,,   ,,   ,,   Elizabeth Tregelles, 11, 19.
,, Samuel, and Charlotte Fox, 9, 11.
,,   ,,   Maria Middleton, 9.
,, Samuel Lindoe, and Rachel E. Fox, 9.
,, Sarah, and Joel Cadbury, 11.
,,   ,,   Wm. Dillworth Crewdson, 11.
,,   ,,   Philip Debell, 7, 19.
,, Sarah Charlotte, and Robert N. Fowler, M.P., 12.
,, Sarah Scantlebury, and B. E. Dungan, 21.
,, Sophia, and Henry B. Foot, 10.
,, Susanna Emmett, and George Hatch, 7.
,, Sylvanus, and Mary Sanderson, 9.
,, Tabitha, and Wm. Cookworthy, *née* Fox, 8, 11.
,,   ,,   Wm. Reynolds Lloyd, 8.
,, Theodore, and Harriet Howell Kirkbride, 12.
,, Thomas, and Catherine Alexander, 9.
,,   ,,   Sarah Maria Howard, 9.
,,   ,,   Sarah Smith, 8.
,, Thomas Were, and Eliza Grigg, 11.
,,   ,,   ,,   Frances Mary Hole, 11.
,,   ,,   ,,   Mary Tregelles, 11, 19.
,, Washington, and Mary Desmond Coffin, 14.
,, William, and Elizabeth Cosserat, 12.
,,   ,,   Tabitha Fox, 8, 11.
,,   ,,   Elizabeth Howard, 11.
,,   ,,   Elizabeth Windeatt, 12.
,, Rev. William Chas., and Eliza Frances Hunt, 14.
,,   ,,   ,,   Georgina Sarah Wodehouse, 14.
,, William Edward, and Emma Molyneux, 14.
,, William Francis, and Charlotte P. Hingston, 9, 19.
,, Dr. Wilson, and Emily Anne Doyle, 9.
Freeman, William, and Harriet Collier, 16.
George, William E., and Elizabeth Ellicot, 22.
Gibbins, Henry B., and Rachel A. Fox, 10.
,, William, and Elizabeth T. Fox, 11.
Gilbert, Elizabeth, and Henry H. Fox, 14.
Gilkes, Alfred, and Sophia P. Hingston, 19.
,, Gilbert, and Louisa E. Hingston, 19.
Goodeve, William, and Elizabeth A. Fox, 15.
Goodwin, Maria, and Edward Bevan, 8.
Gotsall, Maria, and John Wild de Horne, 17.
Grace, James, and Frances Anne Crouch, 7.
Graham, Emily Ellen, and Capt. W. S. Cookworthy, 18.
Grigg, Eliza, and Thomas Were Fox, 11.
,, Maria, and James Fox, 15.
Gwin, John, and Anne Fox, 6.
Hamilton, Sarah, and Charles Fox Hinton, 15.
Hancock, Elizabeth, and J. Folle, 20.

Hancock, Joshua, and Mary Cloak, 6.
   „   William, and Edith Debell, 19.
   „   „   Abigail Tuckett, 19, 20.
Harris, Eleanor, and Philip D. Tuckett, 20.
   „   Mary Elizabeth, and Mortimer J. Collier, 16.
   „   Mary J., and Rev. Alfred N. Hingston, 19.
Harvey, Sarah, and Jonathan Ellicot, 22.
Hatch, George, and Susanna E. Fox, 7.
Helton, Jane C., and John Tuckett, 20.
Hemming, ———, and Eleanor Berry, 6.
Herapath, Alfred N., and Elizabeth H. Matravers, 8.
Hewes, John, and Rachel Ellicot, 22.
Higman, Elizabeth, and Benjamin Fox, 7.
Hill, Arthur J., and Fanny C. Hingston, 19.
Hinds, Honor, and Nicholas Elliott, 6.
Hingston, Alfred, and Mary B. Nottage, 19.
   „   Rev. Alfred N., and Mary J. Harris, 19.
   „   Catharine Tregelles, and Wm. Browne, 19.
   „   Charles, M.D., and Mary Braithwaite, 19.
   „   „   Louisa Jane Parker, 19.
   „   Charlotte P., and William F. Fox, 9, 19.
   „   Dorothy, and Robert Were Fox, 10, 18.
   „   Elizabeth, and Joseph Fox, 12.
   „   Ernest Alison, and Mary E. Davis, 19.
   „   Fanny Catherine, and Arthur J. Hill, 19.
   „   John, and Rachel Collier, 16, 18.
   „   „   Rachel Fox, 11, 18.
   „   Joseph, and Sarah Ball, 18.
   „   „   Elizabeth T. Kenway, 18.
   „   „   Catharine P. Tregelles, 18.
   „   Joseph Tregelles, and Emily Smith, 19.
   „   Josephine, and Robert Dymond, 18.
   „   Louisa Ellen, and Gilbert Gilkes, 19.
   „   Mary, and William Collier, 16.
   „   Rachel Collier, and George Fox, 10, 19.
   „   Rosette, and Reginald Dewing, 19.
   „   Sarah, and Joseph Tregelles, 19.
   „   Sarah Ball, and Walter Prideaux, 17, 18.
   „   Sophia Price, and Alfred Gilkes, 19.
Hinton, Alfred, and Jane Applebee Clark, 15.
   „   Caroline, and Thos. Perrott, 15.
   „   Chas. Fox, and Sarah Hamilton, 15.
   „   John, and Amy Hutchins, 15.
   „   John Lawrence, and Deborah Clark, 15.
Hodge, George, and Rachel Fox, 6.
Hodgkin, Elizabeth, and Alfred Waterhouse, 8.
   „   Thomas, and Lucy A. Fox, 12.
Hole, Frances Mary, and Thomas Were Fox, 11.
Holland, John, and Frances Fox M'Donald, 7.
Hopkinson, Cassender, and John Ellicot, 23.
De Horne, Abraham, and Eliza Butler, 17.
   „   „   Mary Collier, 16, 17.
   „   „   Mary Wild, 17.
   „   Ada, and John C. Todd, 17.
   „   Benjamin C., and Mary Huntley, 17.
   „   Emily, and Henry W. Best, 17.
   „   George, and Sarah Blewett, 17.
   „   John and Sarah Manning, 17.
   „   John Wild, and Maria Gotsall, 17.
   „   Katharine, and Alfred Smith, 17.
   „   Katharine C., and Geo. Bevington, 17.
   „   Louisa, and Alexr. Bevington, 17.
   „   Mary, and D. de Berdt Hovell, 17.
   „   Rosalind, and Edmund Phillips, 17.
   „   Sarah, and John Christy, 17
   „   „   Capt. Hy. Festing, 17.
   „   Thomas, and Emma Johnson, 17.
Hovell, Dennis de Berdt, and Mary de Horne, 17.
Howard, Caroline, and William Matravers, 8.
   „   Eliot, and Charlotte F. Tuckett, 20.

Howard, Elizabeth, and William Fox, 11.
   „   Robert Luke, and Henrietta M. Fox, 9.
   „   Sarah Maria, and Thomas Fox, 9.
Hunt, Eliza Frances, and Rev. William C. Fox, 14.
Huntley, Mary, and Benjamin C. de Horne, 17.
Hustler, Sarah, and Charles Fox, 11.
Hutchins, Amy, and John Hinton, 15.
Irvine, ———, and John Ellicot Carey, 23.
Jackson, Charlotte, and Francis Fox, 10.
   „   Clement, and Elizabeth Emmett, 22.
   „   Eliphaz, and Hannah Westcombe, 22.
   „   Frances, and John Hingston Fox, 10.
   „   Lucy, and Wm. Enoch, 22.
James, Charlotte M., and Jno. Brown James, 16.
   „   Edward, and Charlotte Collier, 18.
   „   Frances and George Fox, 7.
   „   Frances A. J., and Jno. F. Collier, 16.
   „   John Brown, and Charlotte M. James, 16.
   „   Silvanus, and Elizabeth Eliott, 13.
Janson, Margaret, and John N. Smith, 16.
   „   Mary, and George Stacey, 16.
   „   Jane Eliza, and Saml. Lloyd, 16.
   „   John Wm., and Louisa Burnand, 16.
   „   William, and Eliza Jane Dearman, 16.
Jarvis, Emma, and Cornelius Fox, 7.
Jenner, Frances A. J., and John F. Collier, 16.
Jennings, Juliana E., and Francis D. Fox, 15.
Jewell, Margaret, and Charles Fox, 7.
Johnson, Emma, and Thomas de Horne, 17.
Jones, Harriet, and Henry H. Fox, 14.
Kale, William, and Mary Tuckett, 20.
Kealy, Charles, and Flora M'Donald, 7.
Kekewich, Dorothy, and Francis Fox, 6.
Kemmis, Captain William, and Ellen G. de Horne C. Steinman, 17.
Kenway, Elizabeth T., and Joseph Hingston, 18.
Ker, Isabella, and Edward Long Fox, 14.
Kerswill, Anna M., and Charles James Fox, 7.
Kidder, Ann, and John de Horne Christy, 17.
Kiernan, George S., and Louisa Mary Fox, 15.
King, Francis, and Elizabeth Taber, 22.
   „   Joseph, and Tacy Ellicot, 22.
Kirkbride, Harriet H., and Theodore Fox, 12.
Lawrence, Elizabeth L., and Rev. Walter A. Prideaux, 17.
   „   Jonathan C., and Maria L. Chapline, 21.
Leash, John A., and Julia U. Dungan, 22.
Lee, Thomas, and Elizabeth Ellicot, 23.
Leiper, Martha, and Thomas Carey, 23.
Lemmon, Susan G., and Charles James Dungan, 21.
Lloyd, George Braithwaite, and Mary Dearman, 16.
   „   Samuel, and Jane Eliza Janson, 16.
   „   Sarah, and Alfred Fox, 12.
   „   William Reynolds, and Tabitha Fox, 8.
Lorentz, Landorria, and Josiah Fox Curtis, 21.
Lucas, Ellen, and Charles Joseph Fox, 14.
Lugger, ———, and Joseph C. Cookworthy, 18.
McDonald, Frances Fox, and John Holland, 7.
   „   Flora, and Chas. Kealy, 7.
   „   Mary Tabor, and Wm. Ayre, 7.
   „   Thomas Wallis, and Jane Fox, 7.
   „   „   Louisa Baskerville, 7.
MacFadon, Emily, and Andrew Ellicot, 22.
   „   Louis, and Thomas Ellicot, 22.
Macpherson, Isaac, and Tacy Ellicot, 22.
Mairs, Emma, and Walter P. Pridham, 18.
Mann, Jane, and Samuel Eliott, 13.
Manning, Sarah, and John de Horne, 17.
Mason, Elizabeth, and Thomas B. Clark, 15.
Matravers, Edward, and Emma Crawley, 8.
   „   Elizabeth H., and Alfred N. Herapath, 8.
   „   Jno. Howard, and Mary E. Overbury, 8.

Matravers, Lucy, and Ernest Awdry Stiles, 8.
„ Thomas, and Mary W. Percy, 8.
„ William, and Elizabeth Fox, 8.
„ Caroline Howard, 8.
Matthews, William, and Rebecca Allen, 13.
Menhennit, Johannah, and Edward Fox, 10.
Merchant, Sarah, and Elias Tuckett, 20.
Mewburn, Elizabeth Mary, and Rev. C. Wordsworth, 7.
„ George F. B., and Margt. Aitkins, 7.
„ Hannah F., and Rev. W. Toms, 7.
„ Henry ——, and Hannah Fox, 7.
„ Margaret, and Richd. Sargent, 7.
Middleton, Maria, and Samuel Fox, 9.
Miller, Anna, and Josiah Fox, 15.
„ Mary, and Thomas Ellicot, 22.
Mills, Hester, and Francis Fox, 13.
Mitchell, Mary, and John Ellicot, 22.
Molyneux, Emma, and William E. Fox, 14.
Morehead, J., and Catherine Fox, 10.
Morris, Agnes, and Henry Prideaux, 17.
„ Sarah, and Jacob Cookworthy, 18.
Motte, ——, and Maria Davis, 14.
Muller, Charles L., and Mary B. Fox, 14.
Newsom, Sarah Anne, and George F. Fox, 10.
Norris, Lloyd, and Sarah E. Tyson, 22.
Norton, Samuel P., and Mary A. P. Chapline, 20.
Nottage, Mary B., and Alfred Hingston, 19.
Oldham, Wylie H., and Mary Curtis, 21.
Orme, Olivia Blanche, and Howard Fox, 12.
Ormiston, Isabella, and Philip Fox, 12.
Overbury, Mary E., and Jno. H. Matravers, 8.
Padley, Martha, and Jno. Collier, 16.
Parker, Louisa Jane, and Charles Hingston, M.D., 19.
Patterson, Helen, and Philip B. Fox, 10.
Peake, Mary, and Robert Debell, 19.
Pease, John William, and Helen M. Fox, 12.
„ Joseph Whitwell, M.P., and Mary Fox, 12.
Peirce, Joseph, and Emma Fox, 10.
Percy, Mary W., and Thomas Matravers, 8.
Perrott, Thomas, and Caroline Hinton, 15.
Peters, Charles, and Anna Tregelles, 19.
„ Elizabeth, and Joseph Fox, 12, 13, 19.
Phillips, Edmund, and Rosalind de Horne, 17.
„ Ellen, and Alexander Fox, 13.
Pickering, Anna M., and Dillon Pickering, 21.
„ Dillon, and Anna M. Pickering, 21.
„ Elijah, and Rebecca Fox, 21.
„ Henry F., and Hannah Cook, 21.
„ Josiah F., and Rebecca J. Coppock, 21.
„ Sarah F., and Wm. Hy. Seaman, 21.
Pigott, Elizabeth A., and Edwin F. Fox, 14.
Pike, Joseph, and Amy Collier, 16.
Pipon, Edith P., and Capt. Pownall, 16.
„ Col. James K., and Elizabeth A. Collier, 16.
Pitt, Amelia, and Chas. Jas. Fox, 12.
Pomeroy, Cora, and Grafton D. Rogers, 20.
„ Josiah W., and Mary A. Chapline, 20.
Porrett, Emma, and Jno. Collier, 16.
Potts, Nina, and Alphonso F. Tilden, 21.
„ Percival M., and Elizabeth G. Chapline, 21.
Pownall, Capt., and Edith P. Pipon, 16.
Price, Peter, and Anna Tregelles, 19.
Prideaux, Alfred, and Ann Vivian, 17.
„ Charles, and Elizabeth Abbott, 17.
„ „ Elizabeth Wakefield, 17.
„ Dorothy, and Samuel Tregelles, 18.
„ Ellen E., and Lieut. Wace, R.A., 17.
„ Emily Ball, and Francis C. Ball, 18.
„ Frederick, and Fanny Ball, 18.
„ George, and Anna Cookworthy, 17.

Prideaux, Henry, and Agnes Morris, 17.
„ John, and Lydia Fox, 15.
„ Julia Anne, and George Samuel Collins, 18.
„ Philip C., and Esther Bawden, 17, 20.
„ Rachel C., and Robert W. Fox, 10, 18.
„ Sarah, and Robert P. Fox, 8, 18.
„ Sarah Anna, and S. P. Tregelles, 18.
„ Susan Rachel, and Charles Pridham, 18.
„ Walter, and Sarah Ball Hingston, 17, 18.
„ „ Elizabeth Williams, 17.
„ Rev. Walter Alfred, and Elizabeth L. Lawrence, 17.
„ William, and Mary Cowles Anstice, 17.
Pridham, Charles, and Susan R. Prideaux, 18.
„ Walter P., and Emma Mairs, 18.
Puckle, Jane, and Matravers H. C. B. Steinman, 17.
Pulteney, ——, and William Ellicot, 22.
Ramsay, C., and Edith Toms, 7.
Randall, Mary, and William Evans, 22.
Rawes, Anna, and Thomas Thompson, 13.
„ Eleanor, and George Fox, 7.
„ William, and Anna Fox, 13.
Read, John, and Wilmoth Debell, 19.
„ Marie S., and William Bevan, 8.
Record, Elizabeth, and James Fox, 6.
Redmayne, George T., and Katharine Waterhouse, 8.
Reynolds, Katharine, and Benjamin Collier, 16.
Rice, James, and Rebecca Derry, 6.
„ John, and Mary Elliott, 6.
Richards, Edward, and Mary Ford, 6.
Richardson, Jane W., and George E. Fox, 10.
Riggs, Cynthia A., and George D. Curtis, 21.
Ring, Sarah, and Frederick Cookworthy, 18.
Robbins, Charles P., and Rowena C. Caldwell, 21.
Robins, Mary, and Joseph Cookworthy, 18.
Roby, Thomas B., and Josephine I. Chapline, 21.
Rogers, Grafton D., and Cora Pomeroy, 20.
Rose, Rose Isabella, and Right Hon. Sir Robert Porrett Collier, Knt., 16.
Russell, Mary C., and Henry Fox, 11.
Sanderson, Rev. A. P., and Edith Cookworthy, 18.
„ John, and Anna Fox, 9.
„ Mary, and Silvanus Fox, 9.
Sansom, Anne, and Francis Fox, 7.
Sargent, Richard, and Margaret Newburn, 7.
Scantlebury, Hannah, and Francis Fox, 6.
Seaman, William Henry, and Sarah F. Pickering, 21.
Sessions, Joseph James, and Charlotte Fox, 10.
Simmonds, Miriam, and Octavius A. Fox, 10.
Simpson, Ellin, and George F. Fox, 14.
Smith, Alfred, and Katharine de Horne, 17.
„ Emily, and Joseph Tregelles Hingston, 19.
„ Joan, and Francis Fox, 6.
„ John, and Elizabeth Tyson, 23.
„ John Nathaniel, and Margaret Janson, 16.
„ Maria de Horne, and W. Woodward, 17.
„ Rebecca, and Samuel Tregelles, 19.
„ Sarah, and Thomas Fox, 8.
Soady, Anna, and Philip Debell, 19.
„ Rachel, and John Tuckett, 20.
Southall, William, and Elizabeth Allen, 13.
Sparkes, Rachel, and Thomas Binns, 20.
„ ——, and James Tuckett, 19.
Spicer, Charlotte, and John Cookworthy, 18.
Spurrell, Julia S., and Edward Christy, 17.
Stacey, George, and Mary Janson, 16.
Stanton, Frederick, and Jane R. Stanton, 21.
„ Jane R., and Frederick Stanton, 21.
„ Robert, and Jane Ralph Chapline, 21.
Steevens, Rebecca, and John Fox, 15.
Steinman, Ellen G. de Horne C., and Captain William Kemmis, 17.

Steinman, George Steinman, and Emma C. C. Christy, 17.
„   Matravers H. C. B., and Jane H. Puckle, 17.
Stephens, Fanny, and Henry T. Fox, 7.
„   Mary, and John Debell, 19.
Stiles, Ernest Awdry, and Lucy Matravers, 8.
Sturge, Mary Ann, and John Eliott, 13.
„   Sarah, and Robert Were Fox, 10.
Taber, Elizabeth, and Francis King, 22.
Tawney, Charles H., and Constance C. Fox, 14.
Taylor, Henry W., and Elizabeth T. Fox, 7.
Thöl, Georgina E. C., and Edwin Waterhouse, 8.
Thomas, Dr., and Martha Carey, 23.
„   H., and James Ellicot, 22.
„   Margaret S., and Moses W. Chapline, 20.
„   Mary, and Elias Ellicot, 22.
„   W. G., and Mary Wethered, 22.
„   ——, and John Wethered, 22.
Thompson, Alice, and Joseph Eliott, 13.
„   Thomas, and Anna Rawes, 13.
Tilden, Alphonso F., and Sophia Jane Chapline, 21.
„   „   „   Nina Potts, 21.
Todd, John C., and Ada de Horne, 17.
Todhunter, Mary Ann, and Samuel Ellicot, 22.
Toms, Edith, and C. Ramsay, 7.
„   Rev. W., and Hannah F. Newburn, 7.
Treffry, Sarah, and Benjamin Fox, 7.
Tregelles, Anna, and Charles Peters, 19.
„   Peter Price, 19.
„   Anna Peters, and Joseph Fox, 13, 19.
„   Catherine P., and Joseph Hingston, 18, 19.
„   Elizabeth, and Robert Were Fox, 11, 19.
„   Joseph, and Mary Debell, 19.
„   „   Sarah Hingston, 19.
„   Mary, and Thomas Were Fox, 11, 19.
„   Nathaniel, and Frances Allen, 13.
„   Samuel, and Dorothy Prideaux, 18, 19.
„   „   Rebecca Smith, 19.
„   Samuel Prideaux, and Sarah A. Prideaux, 18.
„   Sarah Elizabeth, and Joseph H. Fox, 10.
Trelawny, Florence, and Jonathan E. Backhouse, 11.
Treloar, Sophia E., and Cornelius W. Fox, 7.
Tuckett, Abigail, and Jonah Binns, 20.
„   William Hancock, 19, 20.
„   Alfred, and Helen Curtis, 20.
„   Anna, and Jonathan Bawden, 20.
„   Caroline, and William Cross, 20.
„   Charlotte F., and Eliot Howard, 20
„   Edward, and ——, 20.
„   Elias, and Sarah Merchant, 20.
„   Elias Helton, and Martha Bulgin, 20.
„   Elizabeth, and Lieut.-General Douglas Wemyss, 20.
„   Elizabeth F., and W. Fowler, M.P., 20.
„   Francis, and Mariana Fox, 11, 20.
„   James, and Anna Debell, 19, 20.
„   „   Mary Debell, 19, 20.
„   „   —— Sparkes, 19.
„   John, and Hannah Beswick, 20.
„   „   Hannah Bracher, 20.
„   „   Jane C. Helton, 20.
„   „   Rachel Soady, 20.
„   Mariana F., and Joseph H. Fox, 9, 20.

Tuckett, Mary, and William Kale, 20.
„   Philip Debell, and Esther Champion, 20.
„   „   „   Anna Edmunds, 20.
„   „   „   Rachel E. Fox, 12, 20.
„   „   „   Eleanor Harris, 20.
„   „   „   Elizabeth Wright *née* Curtis, 20.
„   William, and Mary Fothergill, 20.
Tunis, Hannah, and Andrew Ellicot, 22.
Tylor, Edward B., and Anna R. Fox, 9.
Tyson, Elizabeth, and John Smith, 23.
„   Nathan, and Martha Ellicot, 23.
„   Sarah E., and Lloyd Norris, 22.
„   Thomas, and Anna Ellicot, 23.
„   „   Mary Ellicot, 23.
„   William, and Sarah Ellicot, 22.
Updegraff, Julianna, and Francis D. Fox, 15.
Urquhart, Jane, and Joseph C. Cookworthy, 18.
Vivian, Ann, and Alfred Prideaux, 17.
Wace, ——, Lieut. R.A., and Ellen E. Prideaux, 17.
Wadge, Richard, and Sarah Debell. 19.
Wadsworth, Frederick, and Ellen F. Crewdson, 8.
Wake, Ada Mary, and George C. Fox, 11.
Wakefield, Elizabeth, and Charles Prideaux, 17.
„   John Edward, and Rachel C. Fox, 9.
Warrington, Ellen E., and Edwin F. Fox, 14.
Waterhouse, Alfred, and Mary Bevan, 8.
„   „   Elizabeth Hodgkin, 8.
„   Edwin, and Georgina E. C. Thöl, 8.
„   Ellen, and Wilson Crewdson. 8.
„   Katharine, and George Tunstal Redmayne, 8.
„   William, and Mary Janet Burges, 8.
Webster, Thomas, Q.C., and Mary F. Cookworthy, 18.
Weeks, Louisa, and Peregrine Wethered, 22.
Wells, Caroline, and Frederick C. Christy, 17.
Wemyss, Lt.-Gen. Douglas, and Elizabeth Tuckett, 20.
Were, Anna, and Edward Fox, 7.
„   Elizabeth, and Berry Fox, 7.
„   „   George Fox, 7.
„   Mary, and George Croker Fox, 11.
„   Nicholas, and Frances Binns, 20.
Westcombe, Hannah, and Eliphaz Jackson, 22.
Wethered, Charles, and —— Bathurst, 22.
„   John, and —— Thomas, 22.
„   Lewin, and Elizabeth Ellicot, 22.
„   Mary, and W. G. Thomas, 22.
„   Peregrine, and Louisa Weeks, 22.
Whipple, Sophy L., and Mortimer J. Collier, 16.
Wild, Mary, and Abraham de Horne, 17.
Willes, Jane Lewes, and Joseph S. Fox, 7.
Williams, Elizabeth, and Walter Prideaux, 17.
„   Grace, and Robert Debell, 19.
Wilmoth, ——, and Philip Debell, 19.
Windeatt, Elizabeth, and William Fox, 12.
Wodehouse, Georgina S., and Rev. W. C. Fox, 14.
Womersley, Rachel, and Francis Fox, 10.
Woodward, W., and Maria de Horne Smith, 17.
Wordsworth, Rev. C., and Elizabeth M. Mewburn, 7.
Wright, Elizabeth, and Philip D. Tuckett, 20.
„   „   John Allen, 13.
Wylie, Margaret, and Edwin Fox, 10.
Young, Catherine, and George Croker Fox, 11.

Lightning Source UK Ltd.
Milton Keynes UK
UKHW050418270223
417717UK00002B/6